BREATHE

A Guide to Coping Mechanisms and Strategies

Dr. Valerie Simpson

BREATHE

A Guide to Coping Mechanisms and Strategies

Dr. Valerie Simpson

This work is a reference to grief and bereavement coping strategies.

Published by Resetforever Ministries Publishing in 2021

Assistant Editors - Elinor Griffis and Alyse Griffis.

Publisher contact:

valerie@resetforever.com

griefsolutions@yahoo.com

Author Dr. Valerie Simpson is available for book signings, book club events, speaking engagements, seminars, panel discussions and conferences.

To arrange appearances, please contact us via our website: Reset Forever Ministries valerie@resetforever.com or email at griefsolutions@yahoo.com or contact us at Reset Forever Ministries Podcast. Anchor.fm/reset forever ministries podcast

ISBN-978-0-0578-81256-4

Dedication To

SHONTELLE MARIE – My beloved niece, you took care of so many others. Phyllis Marie and Jacquelynn – My elder sisters and mentors in my youth. Robert and Sara Mitchell – My beloved parents who provided an exceptional rearing in a Christ-centered, middle-class lifestyle. Aunt Dorothy - Our babysitter. You made growing up so exciting and memorable. Each of you gave me so much, but left me too soon.

Acknowledgments

DANIEL T. SIMPSON – my faithful husband, Veronica Michelle Gibson – a promise fulfilled, Betty Rimson – lifelong friend, Danielle Bascomb for the back cover of this book, Bishop Lambert Gates – for investing confidence in this ministry, and Shanda Golden for the inspiration of the front cover of this book. You all have inspired and supported me amazingly.

Special thanks to Pat McKanic - Author Extraordinaire.

Contents

Preface

IT IS VERY encouraging to see more people reaching out for solutions to grief as opposed to suffering in silence. I am grateful to have been afforded the privilege to support so many families in illness, times of divorce, decline in health, at their time of death, and loved ones left to grieve.

This book is the culmination of life experiences, including a sudden loss of parents, two sisters and a niece. I was not able to say goodbye. The love of an Aunt that lived with us and helped raise us, my paternal grandmother and many more. My journey included the loss of a set of twins early in the pregnancy. A divorce was on the docket, as were health challenges.

Racial disparity, bullying, verbal abuse, and domestic violence are all among the life experiences. Though I remember the way I felt in each crisis, the spiritual pain that crippled me has diminished and I am on course with my goals and the work appointed to me. Brokenness is now in the rearview mirror. How did I cope with it?

I learned to cry myself to sleep when overwhelming circumstances surged. I cried often and for long periods of time.

Prayer and expectation in God prevented meltdowns and suicide. You will understand it better as you read

BREATHE...

Close to 11 years ago, I had an opportunity to attend chaplaincy training, also referred to as Clinical Pastoral Education and obtained two units of clinical experience at a Trauma II hospital, the only hospital in inner-city Detroit. These were six months of supporting high acuity, emergent cases, which resolved the matter of timidity I had.

For the next five years, I would hold the staff position as an Adjunct Chaplain in the City's Heart Hospital, which also supported, the Women's Hospital, Detroit Receiving Hospital, which is the one hospital I heard most police officers insist on being taken to in the event of a crisis. I also supported patients at the Cancer Hospital and the Rehabilitation Institute.

Occasionally, in the event of an absence of their Chaplain, I was called to support Children's Hospital. One might imagine that every age, illness, ethnicity, religion, cultural challenge, and family dynamic is encased in this period. Virtually, it was. After five years, I trained and began volunteer work as a Police Chaplain with the Detroit police department right about the time I accepted a new job as a Hospice Chaplain.

Hospice advanced my Chaplaincy experience, prompting me to pursue and complete a graduate certification in Gerontology.

This would help me understand the spiritual, financial, emotional, and physiological challenges that accompany aging, death and dying. The acuity of my patients piqued my interest in the processes of the human body, leading me to follow authors that were also physicians, such as Atul Guwande,

"Being Mortal." This opened a new quest to understand the intricate functions of the human body down to the molecular level.

I began taking undergraduate medical courses, such as Anatomy and Physiology and Medical Terminology to improve my clinical documentation skills.

Comprehensively, I applied all the competencies of Action Research obtained from my Doctoral degree to Chaplaincy.

Action Research is the methodology for this discipline. It links theory and practice and incorporates several cycles of this methodology to your research. The successful outcome is an innovative change to existing practices.

With that, I will say this book is a fragment of the practices that were employed in my Chaplaincy work, juxtaposed to personal grief and how I have learned to understand myself in grief and in practice. My intention is to pass it on to many of you seeking hope and ways to navigate anxiety, grief, and depression.

For a more enduring usage of this work, *'Breathe,'* is profitable as a routine guide for anyone endeavoring to support others in grief or crises.

Disclaimer: This is not meant or intended to replace any psychiatric or medical support or medication currently prescribed or suggested by said professionals. However, you will find that some, if not all of the information *'Breathe'* lists, effective in helping to manage the suffocating effects ofgrief, in notable proportions.

Natural breath changes the way the mind processes thoughts; oxygen is necessary for clarity. Bodily function, all the way down to the subatomic levels are affected by oxygen levels. We will now discuss the first step in the plan of care {POC}. This always begins with the assessment/triage, followed by active grief, then finding a way around any hindrances to progression, coping mechanisms and strategies. God breathed the breath of life into man, and he became a living {continuing} soul. Genesis 2:7 {KJV} Breath is translated in Hebrew as "inspiration."

Continue to be inspired and you will live forever.

'In whose hand is the soul of every living thing and the breath of all mankind" Job 12:10 (KJV)

BREATHE

Chapter 1 - She's Not Breathing

BARGAINING

THE SURGICAL TEAM and available staff crowded around the patient on the operating table. Something has gone wrong and the patient is no longer breathing. This was a major upset to the staff; surgery had not begun yet. They had little time to prepare for this one.

She was an 18-year-old, African American young woman who was rushed to O.R. from her hospital room. It appears the stitches from abdominal surgery performed, just a couple of days prior had ruptured, and the patient was losing way too much blood rapidly.

Scheduled surgeries had to be postponed and rescheduled. This is an unanticipated crisis. Emergency surgery was ordered stat. The attending physician was on his way and family had been called in.

It is not looking good. The patient was being intravenously anesthetized. The doctors were reading up on the patient's history and discussing the plan of action. That was when a staff member heard the patient utter the words 'I can't breathe.' The voice faded with the second cry, 'can't breathe.' The patient was no longer verbal, but then someone noticed a twitch in the right hand and left foot.

Nurse: Does she have seizures? (It was a distress signal – it was all she had left}

Medical technician: She is not breathing!

The patient's mental status is now altered from panic to euphoria. The thoughts went from, *somebody help me - I can't talk - there is no more air in my lungs -to - all of my friends are going to hear that I died on the operating table.* I cannot even signal distress with my hand and foot any longer

– I am too weak. There is nothing else I can do...

Finally, someone places a manual respiratory device over the patient's mouth and says, 'Okay, Breathe.'

I had no strength. Breathing was not an option or function for me. I was pretty sure death had come until someone began to squeeze this inflated end of the manual device and I could feel the oxygen entering my lungs. This part of the crisis was now over.

Now, the surgery and a long road to recovery were ahead. I can relax now. I had been temporarily deprived of something so precious and taken for granted. New plan of action

{POA}, restart the patient's respiration and proceed to address the crisis that brought her to the O.R. today.

Obviously, that young lady (me) survived. In life, there are experiences, mistakes, and lessons. This experience gave me an unforgettable lesson; life is precious and can, without notice, come down to a single breath.

Sometimes, life-changing events mark the beginning of a turn in life's trajectory. No matter how one may try, when these types of changes come, years of trying and hoping and praying will teach you, some changes are forever.

The surgery scarcely saved my life. Not sure how long I was in surgery or in the recovery room, but the first memory of consciousness I have following the surgery was waking up to the sound of my parent's voices and being in dreadful tormenting pain in my lower abdomen. "I need Jesus."

My father responded – "You sure do. You said the right thing."

He was close to tears; I could hear it. I was still coming from under the anesthesia, so I was in and out of consciousness. The next thing I remember was being in a dimly lit room. Through the darkness and medication - my vision allowed me to focus on the window in the far corner of the room. I was disoriented for a few seconds, but recognized my parents standing there with their backs turned, mom was crying, and dad was comforting her. I must have groaned or gave some audible level of beckoning:

Mom – "Oh, she's waking up…." They rushed over to the bedside. Mom was smiling with tears flowing down her beautiful face and dad just stared and held my hand.

That was it for this encounter. I cannot tell you how many days and nights I had been out. Sometimes I awoke to see my parents sleeping on the sofa and cot at my bedside where another hospital bed would have been.

One night the phone rang, in a calming cordial tone, my father answered it:

Dad – "Hello… yes, this is Valerie's room… My daughter cannot talk right now… She is very sick. Please do not call back and wake her up… Thank you. Good-bye."

The next episode was when the sedation was wearing off enough for me to look at myself and to see how this ordeal had left me.

First, I noticed there were machines on every side of the bed.

There was a tube in my nostril to drain my stomach, there was an IV (intravenous) tube in each arm, a bladder catheter, and tube to drain the pelvic cavity of blood.

Above my head, there was a blood drip.

Additionally, there was a machine monitoring my cardiac activity and blood pressure.

What happened? What 18-year-old wakes up tethered to machines with no recall of how they got there. Mom and dad realized I was waking up and made it to the bedside.

Mom: "We love you, Valerie. You look good."

Dad – "You are doing so much better; you're going to be alright, darling."

A few days later, they began weaning me off of some of the tubes and machines. It was less congested in there. I was verbal again and remembered telling mom what happened before they started the surgery. She did not seem interested in that at the time. She just wanted me to get better. Eventually, they began weaning me off all the tubes and a liquid diet was prescribed. The therapist advised sitting on the side of the bed, but no walking without assistance. The day I sat up for the first time, I was exhausted and fell into my moth- er's arms for comfort. I had been laying in this bed for threeweeks and it was killing me.

The Physical Therapist began the task of getting me ambulatory again. A regular diet was prescribed, and I was walking on my own. Now that I could eat, my medications could be taken in tablet form versus intravenous. My darkest moments were ahead.

I asked the nurses what each pill was for. It did not make sense to take everything handed to me without knowing their purpose. There was one pill, a burgundy pill – every nurse had a different explanation, For some, answers were a bit creative, but it got me to take the pill. I thought something was being kept from me. An African American nurse discreetly asked me if I spoke with my doctor about it and suggested that I have him explain it. I repeated that in my head. The doctor would explain it. That was unsettling.

"I do want to talk with him." The doctor was not on site that day but promised to come in and talk with me the next afternoon. He came just as promised. He was alone, as was I.

When he entered the room, he closed the door. I became numb. A suffocating sensation and fear came over me. I could feel my heart beginning to race. It could not have been clearer that this was bad news.

Doctor - "I know you have questions for me, and we will talk about that but first, how are you today, Valerie?"

Me: "Every day gets better, but no two nurses could give me the same answer about the burgundy pill I get every morning. I was up all night worried about that."

Doctor – "That is what is bothering you most right now, I understand. Well, when you arrived here last month, you were an extremely sick, young lady. Up until recently, we thought you were going to leave in a pine box. It has been a difficult recovery. I reviewed your chart and the progress, and it looks like everything is favorable for discharge in the next week or so. If you continue to progress with no unexpected complications. We do not foresee any so, look forward to getting back to life as normal with a gradual return to responsibilities.

There were two surgeries. In the first one, we had to remove a fallopian tube. The hemorrhaging that brought you here was caused by the ectopic pregnancy. A fertilized egg was embedded in the wall of the left fallopian tube. The fever and sudden loss of consciousness required the tube be removed to save your life."

Me: "Yes, that was one. The other was in the uterus and hopefully will be okay..."

(Silence)

{I feel the numbness returning and the suffocating anxiety is building again.)

Doctor – "Here is where you took a turn for the worse." The doctor had been giving direct eye contact with every word; he leans in and, with a sigh, explains: "When your stitches ruptured, there was a lot of blood loss, so we performed the emergency surgery. Your uterus is tilted and the hope of maintaining a full-term pregnancy was minimal. The removal of a fallopian tube reduced your chances by an additional 50%. However, when we began surgery, we almost lost you. We explained this to your parents. They love you very much and requested we save your life regardless of necessary measures. That was a difficult conversation for both your parents and me. We did everything we could to save the pregnancy, but your bleeding was too severe, we were forced to perform a hysterectomy.

(Pause)

It was pretty touch and go. We told your parents, if they knew anyone that knew how to pray -pray. We did all we could. I don't think you know how bad things really were. I have never seen a case like this in all of my 20 years of practice.

The pill you were inquiring about was to return your hormone level to normal following the surgery. Many of the medications will be discontinued before discharge. But for now, we want to be sure we get you back to good health."

The room was silent. There was no sobbing, just tears and silence. My thoughts: No children. Lord, please. Then I asked the doctor. "Is there any surgery I can have after I get better?" I was sinking deeply into depression; my questions were farfetched and unrealistic. I was grasping for what essentially was false hope. Tears and the sense of "this is too much" consumed me. I was sure, for the moment, this was the finalization of everything that happened from arrival to discharge. So, I gave in to the despair and cried. The doctor stayed with me for a bit of time to assess my emotional status.

Doctor – "We are glad we were able to save your life that was most important and I knew this was going to be too difficult for you to hear in the critical stages of recovery so, I instructed the staff and your parents to allow you to recover before we had this conversation.

Me: "Thank you for saving my life." {Still, unable to control the tears, I just stopped talking.

Dr: This is difficult for me as well and I can see you need to be alone, so I am going to close the door on my way out and instruct the staff to give you some time.

I can have the nurse give you something for anxiety if you wish. Would you like for me to send her in?" No. "I won't need it. Thank you, Dr. Clark."

When the door closed, I cried until I was weak and sleepy. When I awoke, I cried again. There were episodes of depression. As time passed and I was discharged, and for two years,

I would have crying spells. Depression would set in and I became inconsolable.

I was scheduled to get married in a couple of months. My sanctified mother, sanctified mother-in-law and fiance asked why I was not talking about wedding planning. I just did not want to marry him. He was kind enough to tell me he was okay with me not being able to have children.

I just cried. Those words did nothing for me. I wanted children. and wanted him to console me with hope. I was not handling the truth well at all.

The depression was ruining my life and dictating my decisions. I was out of control. Like a 'perfect storm,' destruction was looming. Without explanation, I quit talking about marriage and discontinued taking calls from him or seeing him. His sister said when my name came up around him. He never said anything bad. He just did not say anything – at all.

My grief now begins shifting from depression to bargaining. "I will rekindle my relationship with God. If I had not been obedient, this would never have happened. The hope was, if I were restored to my status as a faithful child of God, I could "ask-and-it-would-be-given." God would miraculously allow me to have children. My own. Because if I did not have children, there would be no grandchildren. I would be a lonely old lady without hope of ever being happy.

Two years later, I did get married – to someone else. He did not mind that I could not have children. He had a good job and was just a couple of years older than I was. He was extremely popular and from a big family. Yep, this was going to work out… WRONG! What was I thinking? Believe me, that is another book.

However, while I was in this 20-year marriage, I asked God for children. I thought to myself, I have to act like I believe God will answer this prayer, so I began to claim it. I told my husband (at the time} I was pregnant; I told my father-in-law and other family as well as church members. The bargaining stage morphed into false hope. There was no pregnancy, and neither would there be. This did not end well, but at least I was able today, as Abraham "I hoped against hope. Romans 4 (KJV)."

In retrospect, since the divorce, there is no common ground between the two of us and I wish him the best in everything.

Twenty-four years had passed since the earth-shattering news from Dr. Clark to the divorce. I was 42 and single with no children. I will tell you; it is not okay that this was my status after all these changes, but I am going to be alright. All three of my sisters let me name at least one of their daughters. Additionally, I now have a faithful husband that brought three daughters and a son into my world. We are the grandparents of eight and each of these souls have enriched my life. God knows how to reward us after the storm passes over.

I can…

BREATHE

In her book, The Five Stages of Grief, Elisabeth Kubler-Ross {1969} explains the phases people typically go through to process their loss. "Indeed, current grief theory asserts that loss often fosters a transition in the bereaved person's sense of self, for better or worse {Neimeyer & Laurie, 2008, p.173}." How are these needs addressed in your life? *'Breathe'* will explore.

1. Denial - a buffer zone that may help you survive the loss. It is normal and healthy and may be the moment you need.

2. Anger – the actuality or reality that your preference was not the outcome. It is common to wonder why, be consumed with how unfair it is and possibly seek to place blame.

3. Bargaining - pleading for things to be different in return or an alternate outcome. Grief through negotiation. There is an entire list of "what if" statements: "what if I would have left the house 5 minutes earlier"or what if I was at the hospital all night: this leads to guilt, blame, anger and potentially relapsing all 5 phases. It is a domino spiraling effect of grieving.This is also known as the "stage of false hope."

4. Depression – Commonly accepted as a form of grief and is immediately associated with grief. Sorrow is so huge that the world seems too small. Feelings ofnumbness, withdrawal, overwhelm, living in a fog, seclusion, suicidal, homicidal and feelings of givingup.

5. Acceptance – Not so much "It's Okay," but I realize what has happened and "I am going to be okay." Expect to continue having good days as well as bad

days in this stage. You may still experience uncontrollably sad days, but there will be more good days than bad days. {Gregory, 2020} For a complete description of each stage, see appendix B.

Chapter 2 - Triage

DENIAL

TRIAGE – (IN MEDICAL USE) the assignment of degrees of urgency to wounds or illnesses to decide the order of treatment of a large number of patients or casualties.

It is late March 2020, a 46-year-old African American woman parks her car in the hospital garage & enters the hospital with visible symptoms of respiratory distress. In general, the narratives go something like this: occasional coughing, febrile, difficulty breathing is noted, the patent is asked to change into a hospital gown – she is being transferred to the 3 Brush, the covid19 care unit. Shortly after her admission, I receive a call from one of her siblings that she was in the hospital and may have contracted this disease.

I grappled with this for a moment. This disease was on the other side of the planet, shockingly, made its way to the west coast and spread to multiple states before arriving here in Michigan. The State had just shut down or was ordered to 'shelter-in-place 3 days ago and now I am facing the mortality of the most outgoing niece I ever had. The call to her cell phone was my only hope of finding out how bad it was. The nurse's station was inundated. Staff was limited and the hospital was not allowing visitors to any unit for any reason. Thankfully, she answered my call, struggling to breathe, but coherent enough to recognize me and tell me how cold she was and how difficult it was to breathe.

Me: You have to get some hot tea and inhale the steam; the virus cannot survive the heat.

Shontelle:" They won't bring it to this unit Auntie, I have to wait until lunch time."

I was able to reach a unit nurse and pleaded for someone to take her tea or something that would supply steam. A tender-hearted nurse put in a special order, but when it arrived, she was trying to sleep. When I did reach her, she said she had to get up to go to the restroom and she could feel water in her lungs and sitting up helped her to breathe better, but she was too out of breath now and needed to lay down. A third call later that afternoon, she sounded muffled. She had been taken off the cannula tube oxygen and placed on a CPAP - her respirations were declining, and it was happening so fast. Shontelle - "Auntie, they said I am going to ICU." (she mayhave been concerned)

Me: "Okay, that means you will get 24-hour care and will be watched closely." (to quell the fear of going on the ventilator, I added) If they put you on a ventilator, your heart won't have to work as hard because the machine will do the work for you and you will be able to rest better and conserve your energy. Try not to talk too much concentrate on relaxing and breathing and I will check back with you. I love you.

Shontelle – "Okay… (audible respiratory distress) I love you too."

That evening she was not answering her phone. Per the nursing station on 3 Brush, she was transferred to ICU.

She is now on a ventilator; no family allowed visits meaning - no familiar voices, no tender care of placing blankets on her or wiping her forehead if she was sweating, the soft-spoken, calming presence of a trusted soul. All these necessities were eliminated due to the Covid-19 restrictions in place. My heart sunk. I held her as a baby laughed at her as a toddler mocking her mother's walk as she followed her around the house. I loved her unique beauty, which was outshined by her strong personality. She was a marvel. But in this moment, all I wanted was for someone to find a moment to put the phone to her ear so she could hear a familiar voice above the noise of the machines around her bed and staff coming in and out for vitals and to administer medication. A voice that would say, we are all here for you. Everyone is praying for you to get better soon. We all love you. Be strong. This will all behind us in time. Just rest and get stronger.

This is a sad story and it only gets worse. This young lady was bereaved of her father 33 years earlier due to a closed head injury that occurred while riding a moped without a helmet. Her mother, my older sister, passed 11 years earlier following a dialysis treatment. Her kidneys failed due to complications with diabetes and hypertension. Her younger sister had just lost her husband to renal failure just four years earlier. We all loved him as a blood relative because he made my niece so happy. We buried him just one week after burying my Aunt. A faithful woman of God and long-time servant at the church she loved so much. It is difficult to have a loved one pass on and a second to pass before final arrangements have been completed for the first. I remember saying, "Lord, help us get through this."

Ten years earlier, and just 10 weeks after the passing of her mother, Shontelle called, panicked and near hysteria to tell me my eldest sister had just passed suddenly with her husband of 39 years, the youngest daughter, and granddaughterat her bedside.

This death was also related to renal failure.

I was at the nail salon when she called with this news. I had to really slow her down to understand what she was saying.

She managed to get it across to me that I had just lost my eldest sister. I became numb and suffered a short period of shock before the reality of losing two sisters in 10 weeks settled in. I was in the middle of a pedicure. I simply leaned back in the chair, no tears, just weary and forlorn. Remembering now, as if it were yesterday, that Shontell sat at the table with my younger sister and I as we ate the meal prepared for the repass, or the dinner following the funeral services for the eldest sister. I was now the eldest of the remaining siblings. I told my sister, "I'm the oldest so, I'm next," my sister replied, "No, it will probably be me" - my niece interrupted; 'uh-uh, I can't believe you two are arguing about who is next," then she laughed at us. Her laughter lightened the mood. In reality, ten years later, she would be the next of us to depart - unthinkable!

This is the niece that laid dying of COVID-19 in an ICU unit. The guardian of a disabled stepsister, the eldest of four children, her home was the place to be at holidays and her strength made her the respected member of immediate family in-lieu of their deceased parents. Additionally, she raised and provided housing and a family environment for a number of teenage girls and worked two jobs to maintain a modest living arrangement for them all.

So many were depending on her. A true example of a family backbone, a selfless incredible human being. This had to mean something if it was possible to be spared on the merits of her generosity and strength. Two nights later, actually, 1:45 am, I received the call, her heart stopped, and they were unable to get it restarted.

I am numb.

This is not fair; it should never have happened to her. Has not this family seen enough tragedy?

We prayed our hearts out and she still died.

I never liked this hospital. They let my niece die.

Anger and resentment spawns blame – someone was responsible:

I guess she was not as important enough to them as some of the other patients. The medical team, actually, the entire hospital, was accountable in my mind

They made the decision to stop trying so hard to save this life, they were overwhelmed, and this patient is more expendable than some of the others.

They could not save everybody, and she did not make their list of survivors.

No tears, just a sense of helplessness, another sad reality I am being forced to accept. I could not do a thing to save her, and now a huge hole is in my heart and in our family. This is painful, beyond words.

She parked her car for the last time, exchanged work clothes for a hospital gown, for the last time, and talked to me before going to ICU for the last time. I told her I love you for the last time and her last words to me were, "I love you too."

DO NOT WAIT

If there have been rifts between you and someone you love, the decision to put off reconciliation is a bad decision. Do not wait or assume it can be done later or that there will be another chance. That is erroneous thinking.

If you are short on time and need to make adjustments, do not make the mistake of removing the kind gestures. Kind words bring healing and may encourage someone to fight another day or to lift their head in hope. They may find the strength to live a little longer, all because you said a kind word.

Consider reprioritizing what really matters the most. A kind word is free of charge and for some people, these wordsare few and far in-between.

A grad school professor once made a statement that stays with me. I believe it was Pastor William Lickty, he said it once, but it remains with me two decades later; "There will be no change until the pain of being the same becomes greater than the pain of change." Those areas of denial, resistance, vain preferences and desire, or stubbornness often require a greater push to move others forward.

Often, assistance is needed to achieve this change, assistance that is not easily endured causes change. If you are a person of reasonable privacy and dignity, requesting help may be difficult. Moving forward means getting past yourself and reaching out. If you have come to this place and have been left below par or deficient, you are likely seeking help from the wrong people, places or institutions or a combination of the three. Keep in mind; a plan has not failed if you are not compliant or following the plan. If you do not follow it, it is not the plan that is not working; you are not working on the plan.

Again, I remind you, the plan of care in this book is to: 1. Triage or assess the problem, 2. Grieve, and 3. Find a way to manage the pain.

Grief is largely spoken of when referencing death and dying, leaving out the various levels of grief a normal day will present.

Most dictionaries will describe grief as the response to loss, particularly to someone or something that has died to which a bond of affection was formed.

Oxford gives the following definition: deep sorrow, especially that caused by someone's death. A second definition addresses a significant acquaintance with the term grief: trouble or annoyance. I will now refer you to the Prophet Daniel, a visionary that was preoccupied by what he had received. "My cogitations much troubled me...." Daniel 7:28(KJV).

During interventions, it is good to know the cogitations that trouble a person most and work your way out from there.

Address the "911" issue and proceed to the other concerns.

The whole person; mind, body, soul, and spirit function together.

When you are presented with the term 'spiritual pain' in the context of this pain management tool, know that we are referring to anything that is non-material, not a part of your physical body. That would include your: mind, soul, and spirit.

Naturally, heart health is tied to what you eat and your lifestyle.This is aside from congenital/hereditary defects. Likewise, be mindful of what you ingest by way of tv programming,music, and the company you are in. These open spaces for the things that uplift and lead to light-heartedness versus heavy-heartedness.

Heart - the seat of your emotions, "keep your heart with all diligence for out of it are the issues of life." Proverbs 4:23 {KJV} The New Living Translation {NLT} may be more useful to you. This same verse reads as follows: "Guard yourheart above all else, for it determines the course of your life."Filter your thoughts. Practice preventing distressing thoughts from consuming your mind. Learn what triggers these thoughts and limit or avoid these triggers as often as possible until your coping strategies improve. Prevent spiraling thoughts.

Mind – Thoughts, reasoning processes. The things you contemplate and dwell on. Your expectations.

This is where contemplation is applied. Think before you act. Consider where the road is leading before heading down that path. Wisdom prevents unnecessary affliction.

Soul – Where the decisions are made. A wise soul will assess the context they are in and apply the activity best suited for the setting. Deem decisions to be proper or improper
- morally and ethically.

The birth of the Harlem Renaissance. In a difficult place, the African American culture of the early to mid-20th century was driven from the deep South and drawn to the Northern and Midwestern regions of the Country, away from Jim Crow laws – to - industry, jobs and hopes for a better life.

Not being received with open arms, most of them landed in slums. The biggest of them was the city of Harlem. Here the artists, actors, musicians, vocalists, writers, and poets of the culture celebrated their resilience through these arts and expressed the injustices they endured. Poets such as Langston Hughes encouraged a push for equality in his poetry. It came out of his soul.

Find a way to use your talents, gifts and anointing to lift others, celebrate triumphs, and publish anticipations of hope.

Spirit – the natural temperament of an individual. Meek, by nature, hasty, judgmental, rash, unkind, passive, controlling, harsh, inquisitive, distrusting, tenderhearted, abrasive, caring, callous... i.e., These can be further explored in Galatianschapter five as either a fruit of the spirit [the pleasantries] or a work of the flesh [misconduct and offenses].

List the characteristics of your spirit. What type of person are you by nature, and what you hope to be?

_____

_____

_____

_____

_____

_____

_____

_____

_____

_____

_____

One can never be destroyed when they learn to be resilient and how to find rest and restoration for the soul. Reference II Corinthians 4:8 We are troubled on every side, yet not distressed; we are perplexed, but not in despair; 9. Persecuted, but not forsaken; cast down, but not destroyed. (KJV) To get started, there are numerous things to consider.

There are many things that cause grief, in addition to death. It is possible for grief to subconsciously drive your decisions and reactions.

Sometimes reactions to what would normally be minor or disappointing can trigger rage. Unexpected reactions occur when tolerance is low. If there are unresolved issues, confront them, process the grief, and find a way to move forward.

"A person without self-control is like a city with broken-down walls." Proverbs 25:28 (NLT)

Clear the menacing thoughts. Unblock thoughts that stir serotonin and dopamine, the "feel good' hormones that are released by engaging in enjoyable activities and thoughts.

When your thoughts are good, your body chemistry reinforces them with pleasantness. {see the 'Confrontation phase' chapter}

Tackling unresolved grief brings change from lengthy periods of anguish, disbelief, blame, unforgiveness, guilt, betrayal, anger, need for an apology, a place to unload rage, anticipatory grief [what will my future be like] unfinished business – the need for relief becomes the light we look for at the end of the tunnel when it will get better.

What troubles you the most?

_____

_____

_____

_____

_____

_____

_____

_____

_____

_____

Does it emanate from your heart, mind, soul, or spirit?

_____

_____

_____

_____

_____

_____

_____

_____

_____

_____

"The spirit of a man will sustain his infirmity, but a broken spirit who can bear. Proverbs 18:14 (KJV)

"The human spirit can endure a sick body, but a crushed spirit, who can bear it? Proverbs 18:14 (NLT)

A crushed spirit is a spirit that is in tremendous pain and needs repair.

Triage: initializing care. Upon arrival at the hospital, a patient is first processed by a triage nurse, this is where the vital signs are documented, and query takes place. You will likely be asked what brought you in today? Where is the pain?When did this begin? This information provides the medical team with the information they need to identify the problem or decide on the next phase of testing and inquiry. Thecycle eventually leads to a diagnosis and the diagnosis leads to a plan of action.

Unfortunately, with grief, it is a bit more complicated.

Sometimes it is subtle - sometimes, it is demanding and boisterous. Mild signs and symptoms of grief can be as simple as a lack of tolerance or frustration. Then, on the other hand, it can be severe and produce anxiety, stress, and depression and hostility.

Grief can be managed on any level. Learn to employ the coping mechanisms and tools that are as close as the front door or right where you sit, within your own body. Coping tools are readily available and, in many cases, free of cost and medications. Be sure to consult your physician and never take medications that have not been prescribed.

Consider the words of Jeremiah, the "Weeping Prophet:"

"The thought of my suffering and homelessness is bitter beyond words." Lamentations 3:19 {NLT}

"I will never forget this awful time, as I grieve over my loss." Lamentations 3:20 {NLT}

"Yet I still dare to hope when I remember this:" Lamentations 3:21 {NLT}

Grief accompanies death as commonly as grief accompanies lack of any sort. For example, when there is a significant void in your life. Grief is present and intrusive with its manytriggers.

Triggers are persons, places, or things that prompt grief. Grief can be debilitating, crippling, suffocating, and can leave you temporarily dysfunctional, so it is important to know the coping strategies or mechanisms that work best and are appropriate for the time and place grief emerges.

If a song triggered your grief, there must be a song that can lift your spirit. It may even be the same song; you just need to redirect your memory to why that song was so meaningful. Those memories are to be savored. Simply by virtue of the multiple experiences you have shared. If there was a person that triggered your grief or a place that weighed you down, there is a person or place that will lift you? If appropriate, revisit those places or that person. Sharing memories often uncover new information. I was out of town when my mother passed. In the process of editing this book, my younger sister told me she visited my mother the day before she passed. She said mom told her,

"I have already talked to God and I am going to die whether you accept it or not." She knew and she was ready for thatnight.

That reinforced what mom told me the last time I walked out of her hospital room. It blessed me, even 27 years later.

Fond memories are capable of producing hope, healing, and laughter, and those involuntary smiles or blushing. Revisit the memories in greater depth. There is a back story to the images in the photo albums and videos.

Exploration deep into the moments and hours preceding and following the video or the moment the picture was snapped hold words, smiles, incidents, and events. Until now, they may have been overshadowed by regret and emptiness. These are jewels and need to be treasured and protected.

BREATHE

We place our sacred possessions in a safe place to be preserved. As you would a favored piece from the china cabinet, occasionally retrieve them to be admired. Polish and restorethe luster.

Memories deliver admiration and a sense of connectedness.

Manage spiritual pain by collecting and reorganizing for-gotten and new information that came from another source. Store them in your heart and recall them to help counteract heaviness.

I pray these treasures and jewels are never taken from you. Whether present in my life or passed from my sight, as in the case of my parents, older sisters, Aunt and niece, inseparable.

Consider the words of Jeremiah, the "Weeping Prophet:" "It is of the LORD'S mercies that we are not consumed, because his compassions fail not. They are new every morning: great is thy faithfulness." Lamentations 3:22-23 {KJV}Manage feelings of helplessness and hopelessness, by understanding that grief is like an injury to the body: initially-ly, the pain may be extremely sharp and stagger you. But intime and with treatment, the pain is reduced, and crisis levelscan be diminished and manageable. Not time alone, but time and effort.

One of the first steps in suppressing grief, or managing spiritual pain, is to triage the mind. What thoughts are dominating this moment? What are the merits of these thoughts? Do I have to face them or is it something that does not imposean immediate threat to me?

Concerning Covid-19, we recognize the cause of death – just as any other unexpected deaths, generate a powerful shock - like a blow to the body - to those left behind, allowing very little time for survivors to take in the magnitude of their loss. Some experts refer to us as "secondary victims. (Corr, 2001)"

Decompress {release} and Compose {relax}

In death-related grief, the trauma is so severe that it is difficult to begin to control your emotions, tears, and despair. It may go as far as to make you think you are losing your mind. This is a normal response because you are struggling to maintain control. The need for relief could not be greater.

Questions arise such as, how long will it hurt this bad? Will I ever get back to the person I was before the tragedy? Why did this even have to happen?

These thoughts are invasive and dominant, leading to another collapse of control. When these things begin to unfold, acknowledge what has happened, acknowledge what has happened, again, acknowledge what has happened, give it your attention with all sobriety and take it in. PERMIT grief to occur organically. Resisting and suppressing grief is like allowing a wound or boil to fester. Eventually, there will be an eruption. Crying will not emasculate or weaken you. Pressure is escalating, and you would benefit by this decompression exercise.

Cry if you feel the need to.

When you notice a sense of release and relief, even in the slightest measure, relax and enjoy whatever relief you were able to achieve. Be advised that these moments may come and go. It may even seem like you have not gained any ground in the process and you may even want to abandon this coping mechanism, there are others, but I want you to get the full benefit here:

There is a gift incased in the intensity of your grief. Grief has a powerful driving force behind it. Use the intensity of your grief to unload your request to God in prayer. "The effectual fervent prayer of a righteous man availeth much.

When King Hezekiah received the news that he was going to die and not live, filled with heaviness, he turned his face to the wall, prayed, and poured his heart and soul out to God.

Hezekiah turned the tears over to God in prayer. It was such a passionate prayer that God sent the Prophet Isaiah to tell Hezekiah his prayer had been heard and 15 years were being added to his life. The story is recorded in the book of the prophet Isaiah in the 38th chapter.

In recent years, on my job in the capacity of a hospital chaplain, while making routine rounds at the hospital, a unit nurse that was familiar with me asked if I would visit an extremely ill patient. Without hesitation, I took the name and room number of the patient. Upon arrival to her room, I found the patient was alone. She had no roommate and was assigned to the bed furthest from the door.

She spent a lot of time crying, in fear of death and suffering with unmanageable pain. My first inclination was to offer compassionate listening and allow the patient to express her despair. And she did. It was all centered on the unceasing agony her disease caused.

It appeared that the patient was so driven by pain and desperation for relief that she would take extra measures to regain comfort. She had not slept in over 24 hours, and she just wanted someone to help her.

It was this story of Hezekiah that came to mind. So, I told it to her. I added, "What you have to do is turn to the wall, imagine yourself speaking directly to God face to face. Tell Him exactly what you are feeling in your body and your heart. Then tell Him what you want Him to do about it. "So, the prayer went out with fervency and tears. "Lord, I am so sorry, please help me, it hurts so bad and nobody can help me. I need You. Please, Lord, I can't be in here hurting like this." somewhere just beyond those words, she began a beautiful language in her prayer, yes, in tongues. I noticed that her voice began to fade and slow down, then finally, she fell asleep. In a return visit the next day, she was better and had been praying intensely as a means of relief. Another return visits a couple of days later – her room was empty. Hesitantly, I checked with at the nursing station, I learned the patient's pain level was managed and her vitals were stable, and she was well enough to be discharged. She had been discharged to home.

Consider her approach in prayer. She was in anguish and distress. She spoke to Him in the most direct terms. She was direct and she was reverent. He answered. It is important to respectfully approach God and it is beneficial to pour out your heart.

Jesus is a great High Priest; we are informed that our infirmities move Him, they move His heart, His hand and in this case, I witnessed the moving of His Spirit in her. I will never waste time debating what my eyes have seen, and my ears have heard.

Decompression worked for her. And we can all say Amen.

Because tears are a release, in some cases, there will be times when weeping turns into lamenting: heavy sobbing, audible unintelligible interjections that can go on for long periods of time.

Grief is unique to each person's relationship with the deceased and is acceptable if it is healthy grieving.

Unapologetically engage, but tears should not be your only mechanism for coping with grief.

Corona has changed the way we live, die, and grieve. It is unreasonable to dictate another person's method of grieving. However, do keep in mind that this level of grieving for extremely long periods of time and numerous times in a day tend to place stress on the body. When necessary, as much as possible, compose in small increments. An abrupt halt will likely be difficult and unsuccessful. There is no prescribed or allotted time frame. Just keep the process factor in mind.

With time you will move on to milder expressions of grief. Remember, you are processing grief for the sake of release. To move forward, you will need to learn methods of composing yourself after these episodes. By doing so you are regaining control of the emotions and managing your grief journey.

You must resume and continue to achieve goals, dreams, and aspirations. Those do not have to be abandoned. Even if your loved one was a part of those plans, let's talk about legacy projects. (Contact the writer for a personalized legacy project)

Acknowledge, grieve, and find a way around spiritual pain so you can move forward. You will never cease to miss your loved ones, but the pain will not always be as sharp, and heaviness will become lighter.

You are not expected to forget this bond of effect they provided. Neither is it encouraging. But the bond will continue toexist in different ways.

Re-experience good and loving memories, expect laughter and even blushing to return and yes, you will have moments of laughter. Do not be surprised if critical statements emerge. This is all a part of recall and reckoning - all within the collection of memories.

Chapter 3 - Complicated Grief

FEAR

SOMETIME AGO, I was engaged in an intervention with a young lady that admitted suffering with depression that was getting beyond her coping range. Also, termed "grievingparameters (Simpson, 2016)."

Initially, it was apparent that she needed a platform to voice her grief. The intervention went as expected and revealed she had quite a bit on her mind. All her complaints were concerning and needed to be heard. The call started as a monologue; she had the liberty to speak candidly. After a reasonably short period of time, she transitioned from expressing her concerns to becoming increasingly irritable as she told me of her disparities.

Her narrative soon shifted to betrayal, then anger.

I noted she conveyed victimization from many, including immediate family. Sadness immerged. Finally, her voice escalated and accelerated.

That was when I said, "Okay, now we are going to stop." {we both paused} after a few quiet seconds, I told her to take a breath – just breathe for a moment. It was necessary for her to express her grief; she had been through a number of ordeals and needed someone to give credence to her plight simply by listening. So, the intervention was {1} listen, listen patiently and compassionately, and {2} breathe. Change in respiration is a clear sign that physiological changes are being triggered from her grief, and there was no better time to learn to regain control.

As a hospital chaplain, I learned that respiration and heart- rates are monitored and controlled with medication if necessary.

Elevated respirations are indications of pain in non-verbal or subconscious patients. It is among signs and symptoms that a chaplain is to bring to the attention of a doctor or nurse and document it as part of the intervention. Perspiration is also a symptom of pain and anxiety in non-verbal patients.

This is monitored because they cannot speak for themselves.

In this intervention, the young lady was experiencing spiritual pain and that triggered the same physiological reactions. It is the body's way of calling for backup help to get the normal functions realigned. Breathe.

Self-care tip:

Breathe- it slows the heart rate to calmer normal ranges. Breathe- it carries oxygen to the brain that can clear brain fog and confusion. Breathe - it is a moment to collect your thoughts, affirm reality and take corrective measures. If conditions permit, a walk outdoors or even just stepping outside for pure oxygen versus recycled, climate-controlled air is much better and almost immediately realized. Breathe.

Self-care tip:

If time and conditions permit, stop for a few moments of self-care. Step outside; if you are at work, take a walk down the corridor or to the breakroom and back. If this is not possible, grab a bottle of water and pause. The water will carry a supply of oxygen to the brain, other organs, and muscles, refreshing the body just enough for a reprieve and to recompose.

Self-care tip:

Selfcare is simple and does not have to be time-consuming. For every 20-minute segment of mental relaxation {dismiss thoughts of obligations and demands}, the mind will be rewarded with an additional 2.5 to 3 hours of intensive focus as needed. Stretch the limbs, relax the shoulders, look at the clouds feel the breeze. Even a small portable fan provides comforting sensations.

Research studies from the Department of Health at the University of Mississippi concluded that breathing interventions.

demonstrate the ability to lower blood pressure, lower cortisol levels, increase serotonin levels, and reduce anxiety as well as lower depression. (lower serotonin levels can result in mood disorders such as anxiety or depression. {Scaccia, 2020}

Please document your experience from these self-care exercises.

_____

_____

_____

_____

_____

_____

_____

_____

_____

_____

_____

_____

_____

_____

_____

_____

_____

_____

_____

_____

Chapter 4 - Detoxification

ANGER

THIS CHAPTER WILL present the most challenging task you will be asked to complete, and as God would have it, this task will present the most valuable rewards in your healing process.

A dentist will not extract a tooth in an abscessed socket. Patients at most hospitals are given laxatives to eliminate toxins. To advance with God, you must admit and address spiritual toxins. You will feel so much better, even physically. You will thrive better and lengthen your life by getting rid of the toxins.

The brain sends neurotransmitters to organs that will release natural chemicals in the body to regulate activities in the body like stress, respirations, and hypertension. But if the body is full of toxins and other foreign substances, the receptor sites may have a film on them, reducing the effects of these messengers. You will need that corrected for the body to operate efficiently and immediately.

Detoxification suggests there are foreign substances or agents that the body must be ridden of.

When this step is neglected, toxins multiply, traveling through the bloodstream and eventually, every tissue, will be breached by these toxins, organs and their systems, until the entire organism, that is, the entire person, is contaminated and living in a polluted body.

Speaking strictly from a spiritual standpoint.

What are these toxins and how are they disregarded? Jesus said, "It's not what goes into your body that defiles you; you are defiled by what comes from your heart." Mark 7:15 New Living Translation {NLT}

Toxins in our spirit-non-material being {mind, soul, and spirit} waste or the useless residue left behind, sometimes for years after the experience is over. Anger is the stage of grief that damages and destroys neurotransmitters. These chemical messengers are notified by the body's sympathetic nervous system that something is going on in the body that needs to be addressed. They travel down the spine to the gland it was dispatched to. That gland releases hormones directly into the bloodstream and travels through the entire body. Toxins can prohibit and diminish the functions of neurotransmitters.

Anger releases cortisol to help the body deal with stress by raising blood pressure and cortisol levels.

This is effective and only lasts for a short term. They come to aid in immediate times of crisis, after which the levels areto return to normal.

When anger is sustained or is a way of life, the individual lives with elevated cortisol levels for extended periods of time, damaging neurotransmitters, suppressing the immune system, sustaining elevates blood pressure levels and creating health threats.

The first line of defense; keeping your heart and mind on par with constructive thinking and meditation. We are not saying empty your mind and free yourself of thinking. The brain is too powerful for that. But keeping your mind on pleasant thoughts.

Aspirations, hopes, fond memories and even expectations for favorable outcomes in all that you endeavor. These will immediately correct the aforementioned chemical imbalances and reduce the threats. (Read 4:8)

What will help you with that? Doing things that are healthy and safe for your mind-body, spirit, and soul. Protect your life and consume wholesome literature and television programming, music. Surround yourself with people that will build your health with wholesome words and conduct.

If it leaves you with grief, anger, frustration, bitterness, or rage, it is toxic to you. I strongly advise taking a long hard look at whether the people, places, or things I just mentioned leave you with these emotions. Is it your personal feelings about them? Are they eating away at you or are you killing yourself?

Heed the words we read from the book of St. Matthew, "For out of the heart proceed evil thoughts murders, adulteries, fornications, thefts, false witness, blasphemies {slander}:" Matthew 15:19 {KJV}

Without this, your detox efforts could be the equivalent of a band-aid on a bullet wound. It just will not work. I will explain why in a moment. In the meantime: "Consider what I say and The Lord will give you understanding in all things." 2 Timothy 2:7 (KJV)

With so much at stake, we would do well to use every tool offered in this intervention. There is almost always a benefit in our experiences:

And not only so, but we glory in tribulations also: knowing that tribulation worketh patience;

And patience, experience; and experience; hope:

And hope maketh not ashamed; because the love of God is shed abroad in our hearts by the Holy Ghost which is given unto us. Romans 5:3-5 (KJV)

Our Experiences Purify and Fortify Us

So, we can rejoice, too, when we run into problems and trials, for we know that they help us develop endurance.

And endurance develops strength of character, and character strengthens our confident hope of salvation.

And this hope will not lead to disappointment, for we know how dearly God loves us because He has given us the Holy Spirit to fill our hearts with his love. Romans 5:3-5 {NLT}

It is the love of God filling our hearts {vs. 5} that we lack and some people, we may be absent of that love. Hear the words of Jesus concerning toxins or:

"Not that which goeth into the mouth defileth a man; but that which cometh out of the mouth, this defileth a man" Matthew 15:11 {KJV}

"But those things which proceed out of the mouth come forth from the heart, and they defile the man." Matthew 15:18 (KJV)

"For out of the heart proceed evil thoughts murders, adulteries, fornications, thefts, false witness, blasphemies {slan-der}:" Matthew 15:19 {KJV}

"These are the things which defile a man." Matthew 15:20 (KJV)

To be defiled in this context is to be desecrated, rendered ceremonially unclean, and common. For the safety of the rest of the congregation or society, anything ceremonially unclean was to be placed outside of the camp {a form of quarantine} to prevent contamination and further spread these toxins.

So how are these toxins ingested:

Mouth – ingest, most 24-hour viruses are food poisoning – bad food. Pathogens and bacteria are hidden from the naked eye. It may appear harmless and appetizing. The very appearance in a picture, absent of the aroma, can increase your appetite and induce cravings. Essentially, this is poison under the guise of nutrition. The misery is just hours, maybe mere moments ahead. This would be the equivalent of your consumption. Be judicious about what you consume and protectyour life.

In the words of one nutritionist: "We are digging our graves with teeth." It is what was meant when He said: "what goes in a man" Specifically, The Bread of Life or the scriptures that are read to us, taught to us, preached to us and sang to us that equates to good spiritual nutrition. Evil communications corrupt good manners. You do not have to give others the liberty to pump toxins into you. Guard your heart.

Transdermal Absorption- through the skin- wounds {see types of wounds} Pathogens, close associations. You can anticipate what you will get from being in the presence of brawling, bickering, contentious, derogative people. By now, it should grieve your spirit. Continued socialization can desensitize and corrupt your thinking. It is cunning and aggressive. You will find yourself spewing the same ills on others. No one deserves that. These are choices we have to make for our personal mental well-being

Inhalation - sinuses, environment - pathogens in the atmosphere.

This segment is an appeal to those who have suffered betrayal, injustices, abuse {emotional or physical}, bullying, bad divorce, abandonment, undermining, castigation, character assassination and anything that can be associated with these terms.

These are spiritual atrocities that have lasting effects. They leave seeds of bitterness that are watered and spring up with each of life's battles. Chances are, one or more of the above, have happened to us all. (Ecclesiastes 3:1-11)

The residue and toxics must go. This is a Herculean task. It will take heavy lifting to rebuild the structures that have been destroyed, such as trust, hope or confidence. It has been said of some "you can eat the elephant one bite at a time."

The reality is, life is riddled with all the encounters listed above and in the moments of disbelief, anger, vengeance, sorrow and numbness, things are often mishandled. When mishandled, a host of disconnects reactions and deeper levels of pain are spawned. All is not lost; this is not the 'point of no return' even if someone involved has passed on. There is always a way when God is involved.

In preparation for departure, the flight attendant will instruct the passengers on the following

"In the unlikely event of a water landing, be aware of the exit nearest you and take your seat cushion to be used as a floatation device" {she/he will also say} "should the cabin lose air pressure, oxygen masks will drop down in front of you, if you are traveling with a small child, be sure to secure your mask first before assisting the child." [If you have ever flown Southwest Airlines, just to lighten the urgency of that instruction, the flight attendant may add] "if you are traveling with a child or someone acting like one, please secure your mask first before assisting them."

For your safety, sanity, peace of mind, [whichever best fits], we are going to secure ourselves first. So we can breathe.

As with any challenge, the participants are informed of the reward, beforehand, so they will be heartened and empowered to endure to the end and accomplish this goal – over- coming to every hurdle. The reward is, the spiritual bleeding will stop, the wounds will heal, and your peace will be intact. Equally as important as the spiritual reward are the natural ramifications:

Mental health problems such as depression, anxiety, stress, and insomnia are among the most common reasons for individuals to seek treatment with complementary therapies such as yoga. Yoga encourages one to relax, slow the breath, and focus on the present, shifting the balance from the sympathetic nervous system {SNS} also known as the flight-or-fight response, to the parasympathetic system and the relaxation response. The latter is calming and restorative; it lowers breathing and heart rate, decreases blood pressure, lowers cortisol levels, and increases blood flow to the intestines and vital organs. (McCall, 2007)

As a clinician, I do not recommend Yoga as therapy. Yoga is a Buddhist practice, something I know extraordinarily little about.

However, it is not uncommon to experience brief periods of respiratory irregularity due to stress, depression, and anxiety. There is a suffocating effect associated with anxiety attacks. With that, I recommend you focus on respiratory function to achieve relief, as it is a necessary human function. The benefits listed by McCall apply.

My profession has placed me shoulder to shoulder at the bedside of patients with physicians. The intention of the interdisciplinary approach was to identify the spiritual/ immaterial need of the patient and allow the Chaplain to implement spiritual care interventions. Every clinician noted respirations for both verbal and non-verbal patients and the reactions of the patient to the perspective intervention.

Tactile stimuli such as familiar music, familiar voices, and tactile touch therapy, such as softly stroking the arm or brow and familiar fragrances, registered adjustments in blood pressure and respiration, as well as heart rate on the monitors.If the patient is not visibly or measurably responsive to tactile stimuli, as a Chaplain, I would use a pair of glovesavailable to the medical team and brush them across the face,closer to the cheeks or lips. This noxious stimuli is painlessand always works but does prove there is brain activity. Thiswas also documented for the sake of reporting to the inter-disciplinary team.

The point is the proper stimuli proves there is still life there. They are still with us. The goal now is to bring the patient back to functional status.

Protect Your Life

Turning now to the words of Jesus, "You are defiled by what comes out of your heart" Mark 7:28 {NLT}. There are toxins in the spiritual portion of the human species that wreak havoc on every part of your being. They are destructive and deadly.

Though they do not always begin in this advanced state, the outcome is the same. Protect your life by paying attention to the traps. Recognize they have the potential to escalate and choose to avert it. To do that, you simply need to masteryour temperament.

Subtle Tipping Points

Years ago, my husband and I adopted a puppy from a pet supply store. This day an animal rescue shelter was designated to bring in cats and dogs suitable for adoption.

An Australian Shepherd got my attention. He turned out to be a very smart dog, learning to follow commands quickly.

Occasionally, I would take the dog to a pet supply store to pick up supplies and to allow him to intermingle with the other dogs. This allowed me to talk with other owners about their pets and experiences. One such visit, I spoke with a dog trainer that was holding a class in a partially closed-in area in the back of the store. After the session, he was kind enoughto give me a few tips.

Trainer: What is your pet's name?

Me: Mr. Barker.

Trainer: firstly, you may want to change that to one name. He will respond to it easier. (never, I loved the name).

Trainer: Secondly, when you are here and Mr. Barker is reacting to the sights and sounds of other dogs around you, he will follow your lead.

Meaning he would react calmly if I did; he would panic if I did. This strategy works.

Even a pet we now have, Chloe, would panic and hide on the 4th of July in fear of the sound of fireworks. Now when my pet sits up or looks around to see the noise, I softly say a few words - she takes note of the tone and calm and now sits outback and watches the fireworks with no fear. Fight or Flight"

As previously mentioned, consider the level of harm the situation poses to you. Is it safe enough to contend with? Can you conquer it? If so, fight. Is it overwhelming and beyond your ability to contend with right now? In this case, flight would be reasonable. Know your limits on how much you are able to endure. Continue using your coping mechanisms as you learn to manage grief better. It is like building a muscle with time and resistance. Eventually, you will fight. Know your tools and mechanisms.

Consider Your Ways (urgent)

These words are of utmost importance in times of grief when emotions run high and pain runs deep. Master these simple but potent strategies and in turn, you will prevent years of anguish. Families often spend years confronting unresolved and mending relationships snared or damaged in times of grief. The power of life and death are in the tongue, because words carry with them either the seeds of bitterness and gull or comfort and healing.

They can also carry rationality and consolation. Either way, the seeds are planted, by life's experiences. These plants produce the same seeds. We are admonished that a root of bitterness springing up will cause many people to be defiled or tainted. Toxins are passed through them.

Others can be dishonored, corrupted, degraded, violated, debased, besmirched, and contaminated by a single seed with the root of bitterness. Your toxins and mine.

{This will be the discourse of chapter five)

The word "good-bye" is a reference to the words "God be with you." This is a type of blessing, practices speaking blessing on others by way of kind words. We are told to bless even those that hate us, not to curse them.

Speak kindness, speak genuine complimentary words. Season your words with thoughts that preserve psychological and emotional strength.

Blessings are the medicine that detoxifies. Even if the person is nursing bitterness, leave the seeds of worth and dignity behind.

They may take root at some point, but in the meantime, your "feel-good" hormones have been generated by the blessings you spoke so that when you leave their presence, you can...

BREATHE

Practice listening.

Set aside preconceived opinions and listen with compassion in this mental exercise. Listen and remember the words spoken, reactions, responses and take ownership of your responsibility. Perhaps, you are ready for reconciliation now; maybe not. You are not responsible for the response of others, but at least you will have done your part and cleared your conscience.

But consider your ways.

Try to identify toxins and reoccurring related issues

_____

_____

_____

_____

_____

_____

_____

_____

_____

_____

_____

_____

_____

_____

_____

_____

_____

_____

_____

_____

Chapter 5 - Deepening Bonds

ACCEPTANCE

IT HAS BEEN my privilege to serve families in bereavement support groups. Whether the session was at the hospital or a home, often, it occurred in grief support groups hosted by hospitals and hospice organizations. In every discussion these past 11 years, I heard of desire to spend time talking with their loved one, even if it were just for a moment.

This is the most popular desire of loved ones left behind to grieve. Most have resigned themselves to the reality that the event of death has occurred, and it is no longer possible to strengthen that bond– so they mourn this missed opportunity. Imagine being told to "move on" in this fragile state of mind? It happens. It is painful and disorienting. No one ever should be disenfranchised of grief. {Disenfranchised grief in appendix A}

Grief should never be dismissed as insignificant. It is expected to be honored and recognized. This is the initial path to supporting others. Acknowledge this life-changing event. Take time to understand how life's events impact others. Humanity drives us to help wherever we can. Caring is half the battle.

Describe the effect that helping others has on you.

_____

_____

_____

_____

_____

_____

_____

_____

_____

_____

_____

_____

_____

_____

_____

_____

_____

_____

Seeking to deepen the bond shared with your loved one is one of the best ways to embrace what you already have. There is comfort in knowing these bonds can never be taken away. It reverses the sorrowful effect of being visibly detached. You will celebrate the bond. All the more, the bondwill be deepened.

Instead of pursuing detours when grief intensifies, remember you do not always have to avoid it. Rather, use this as an opportunity to explore ways of reconnecting. Having a sense of their presence and permanence can be discovered and the bonds once shared can be deepened. I will share with you a simple, unanticipated answer I received while I was grieving the death of my father, Robert John Mitchell. The first member of our immediate household to pass away.

As previously mentioned, this unanticipated comfort always helped someone in grief interventions and has smoothed sharp edges in many grief journeys through to the healing process.

I will pass on other methods, I may or may not have personally proven, but others have deemed them profitable enoughto pass on. (See the end of this chapter)

Upon the death of my father, I helplessly stood by his bedside as he flatlined the medical equipment showed heart activity stopped. The beeping sound on the heart monitor stopped and a sustained pitch filled my ears and hearts. The mechanical statement that everyone understood, dad's heart just stopped. I was numb.

One of my elder sisters, Jacquelynn, and I were rushed into a private waiting room furnished with a couple of love seats and a few chairs. There was also a phone made available to us for obvious reasons. The doctors were attempting to restart his heart. We were too young for this. How could these 34- and 35-year old women navigate life without their father? But it was so. No tears from me today, but my sister was inconsolable.

This had to be a God-given buffer zone for me. I remember calling our pastor and telling him I thought I would be on the floor in denial over this crisis, but I was amazingly calm.

I proceeded to contact our siblings and my dad's siblings with great apprehension of giving them this difficult news. I worried about how it would hurt them. Of his five siblings, dad himself being the middle child of the six born to Luke and Lila Mitchell, he was the first to pass.

Why no tears? I was a daddy's girl, at his side, always. He was the first of his siblings to die and the first of our immediate household to pass away. This was a milestone for multiple generations - a new level of grief. We were all in uncharted territory.

The tears showed up the day before the funeral and seemed to be in control. I thought they would never stop flowing. Like the other signs of grief that emerged, shock, denial, bargaining, anger, and acceptance, I began to realize how much I was really was like my dad. My personality, my hands, complex- ion, eyes, entrepreneurial quests, accomplishments.

Though these characteristics were obvious for years, they had now become so much more meaningful. I needed to find more ways to identify as he child. He had given me something more valuable than a middle-class rearing, a two-parent household and an introduction to dealing with life itself. We were the fourth generation of our holiness faith tradition on both sides. Yet, I was much more a part of who he was in this world. I was on a quest. Everything that would attach me to him was of major significance, even if it meant identifying with his illnesses or comorbidities-maybe that was "a-bridge-too-far," but it was an attachment and a bond. In the most unlikely way, strangely enough, it seemed to comfort me. So, I examined the features and characteristics we shared. So much and so precious were the things that could never be taken away. Bonding and deepening a truly bonded father-daughter relationship was realized in an obscure and unanticipated form. Recalling stories, he told me of his youth and life took on a deeper meaning.

Spouses and significant others have been said to look just alike, even the ones that have little to no genetic similarities. How were they viewed by even their closest friends and loved ones to look alike? In many cases, they shared the same gestures and offered the same response and facial expressions in social settings. Even quotes, opinions and hobbies revealed their affinities were close or even identical. How so? I wondered. Did one give into the other? Did they learn to understand, favor, and mimic one another? Did opposites attract and agreed to meet in the middle as they matured and became more pliable? I Corinthians 13 makes it clear that love conquers all. Perhaps, it went just the way it was designed to go, and they balanced each other out. Rediscover your similarities and the bond will grow deeper. Treasured advice. Personalized legacy projects are highly recommended.

{Please follow up with the author for suggestions on per-personalized legacy projects}.

Suggestions from theorists.

"Continuing Bonds" theory revolves around the idea that people maintain a relationship with those they have lost. {Continuing Bonds, 1996). "African Americans keep the spiritual bond between the living and the dead strong through cemetery visits, talking with the deceased and having a clear sense of the deceased's presence {Rosenblatt, 2005, p. 215}."Additionally, other experts suggest; writing a letter, planting a tree in their memory, donating in their name, finishing a project they may have started. Whatever it takes…

BREATHE

Chapter 6 - Detached

ANTICIPATORY GRIEF

MY BROTHER CALLED me: "Val, Aunt Dorothy is in the hospital." Me: "Which one?"

Rob: "Sinai, I will visit after work."

Me: "Okay, I have patients there, so I will see her today aswell and I will update you when I know what is going on."

She was awakened by the words,

Me: "Hi, Aunt Dorothy." [She immediately began to cry;she was worried about the severity of her condition].

Me: "What's wrong? Why are you crying? I work out of this hospital sometimes, so I was able to come and visit today."

Aunt Dorothy: "How did you know I was in the hospital? Did somebody tell you I was dying?"

Me: "No, not at all. I am glad to see you, though. What happened?"

Aunt Dorothy: "I had a stroke at the end of church service yesterday and the ambulance brought me here. I have paralysis on my left side, and I get really sleepy sometimes. I told her I would talk with the medical team to get more information."

The team had already decided to perform a procedure.

My question was if they discussed it with my Aunt. She was coherent and competent; it was her decision. I was disturbed by what they had planned without discussion.

Never did they discuss the diagnosis or the severity, or an option to surgery. After further discussion, they canceled the surgery, and I went to discuss it with my Aunt.

No, emphatically not. She would not consent to surgery.

The option was palliative care or hospice. I worked for hospice and knew the level of care she would be receiving on this unit was exceptional and I could spend time with her after my shift and during rounds. Within hours, she was out of the hospital's care and on the hospice unit. A beautiful room on a serene unit with a gentle and skillful staff was on hand day and night. She was loved. Her lethargy increased. She was not opening her eyes now, but responded to questions with a faint yes or no.

Sometimes, when she heard me enter the room, she would extend her hand so I could hold it. Obviously, the night nurse would sit with her and hold her hand. That comforted her. She wanted to live. She was in no wise afraid to die, but she was declining pretty quickly. The staff kept her on the unit until they were able to stabilize her pain medication in a way that would allow her to interact with family and manage her pain at the same time. Someone found out she liked Pepsi. The hospital did not have it, so a staff member purchased a bottle and gave her a few drops. This was refreshing even though she could no longer swallow the flavor of the Pepsi on her tongue was enough to provide pleasure. She continued to decline, but the pain was managed enough for her to be dis- charged to a facility. I selected a facility close to her church for convenient visits from church members. Once that was done, she could be discharged.

I think it was for my sake that they kept her on the unit an extra week so she would get that affection and attention that made the deterioration bearable. At any rate, it was time for her to be discharged. There would be care available around the clock. Arrangements were made with an acceptable nursing facility. She was discharged around 10 pm that night. I found it acceptable among the facilities I had been visiting at in this community. She was discharged around 10 pm that night. I stayed with her for a long time. Later I headed home on the other side of town, about 45 minutes away. I was off the next day and could spend it with Aunt Dorothy and other families. That was the plan. I arrived at 12 noon that day. The first thing I noticed was that the Music Therapist, a true clinician in her discipline, was already at the bedside singing to her.

Music Therapist: "I called you. Her respirations are 44 per minute, she is sweating, and they have not given her oral care yet. I spoke to the nurse's station and called the office to let them know what was going on."

Me: "I appreciate you. Have they given her something for pain yet?" The therapist shakes her head no. We are still waiting.

She is in crisis. She was medicated before leaving the hospital the night before and needed her medication when she woke to stay ahead of the pain. The doctor sent orders for her meds with the ambulance, but the facility pharmacist had not filled them yet. As I would for any of my patients, I visited the nurse's station to speak with the nurse caring for my Aunt. All I got there was that they were waiting for the doctor to send the orders so she can receive her pain meds. "She is sweating and writhing in pain with the little strength she has. Are you able to reach the pharmacist by phone? She also needs oral care. I just want her to be comfortable. We know she won't be with us much longer, but we hope to see her spend it in comfort." Thirty minutes and an hour go by, no meds. Aunt Dorothy is visibly in misery.

She's looking in my eyes as if pleading for me to do something. I did all I could do. The Music Therapist went above and beyond the call of duty, even comforting me, the Chaplain.

I called her pastor. She lived with that family during his childhood, so he knew her like an Aunt. His deceased father made it his business to see that this member of the church was cared for and all needs were provided. That was the kind of man this honorable Bishop was.

But now he was deceased, and the son took up the responsibility of keeping my Aunt under his care. He did not come to the facility when I called, but he sent another church member.

By the time she arrived, Aunt Dorothy was in too much pain for socialization.

I am infuriated and in anticipatory grief witnessing the demise of my mother's baby sister. This facility had not moved quickly enough. One hour and forty-five minutes into my visit, the hospice organization I worked for sent one of our nurses to provide medication in-lieu of what the facility could not seem to issue. They were also sending one of my colleagues, a Chaplain. They wanted this to go from a bad situation to a managed one.

When our nurse arrived, the Music Therapist apologized but had to visit other patients.

The hospice nurse asked me to step out so she could work with Aunt Dorothy.

Thirty minutes later, I was called back into the room. She is still in distress, but I anticipated the medication to make things better really quickly. Her respirations changed; they were labored. Her stare indicated something is wrong, but she could not talk. It was a plea for help. She was clearly transitioning. I held her hand and sang while

providing tactile stimuli. Aunt Dorothy, I asked: 'You love Jesus,' she nodded and stared with intensity. Then she gasped deeply putting her hand to her chest, then a second gasp, a long pause and then she closed her eyes. She was gone. This was a "bad death," as we describe them in our interdisciplinary team meetings.

This lady was like no one I have ever known. She was the youngest of 14 children, my grandfather died when she was an infant, and my grandmother died when she was two years old. These 14 orphans were transferred from one foster care home to another during the great depression. She grew up never really knowing her parents. She never married or had children. But when it came to her local church – she gave them her soul. She had been a janitor, coatroom attendant, office support staff, choir member, and greeter at the church's senior home. She had keys to just about every door in this megachurch building.

My aunt had also been nominated Woman of the Year by her church four times of this 40+ year membership.

When we arrived at the church for the funeral, the halls were lined with so many church members. My heart was lifted. During the services, numerous people came forth to tell how loyal she had been. She was a bit babyish, because her siblings babied her since they were the only parents she knew. The pastor told a hilarious story on how the previous pastor attempted to fire her for stubbornness, by saying:

Bishop: 'Dorothy, give me the keys,'

Aunt Dorothy: 'No.'

That went back and forth a few times before she left the office and he followed her. The church is located on a major the intersection of the city and from the church offices, the intersection is clearly in view. When they left the office, they left the building and were seen at the stoplight waiting for it to change so they could cross back and forth in that intersection. 'Give me the keys' - 'No.' A standoff between two strong personalities. In the end, not only did she remain on staff, but the pastor was there to pick her up from home to bring her to work from 6:30a Monday through Friday. That prepared me for what was to come. One of the saddest things I have ever seen. The funeral procession to her final resting place.

"All of her siblings" had passed. She had no children and never married. When the hearse pulled around to load her casket and to organize the cars for the processional, my husband and I pulled behind it. After several minutes, the funeral director asked,

Director: "Are there any more coming," Me: "No Sir, just the two of us.

The lights were flashing on the hearse. Of course, we had the right of way in all intersections, and we had a funeral flag on our vehicle. Imagine for a moment, the stares from the people on the street and in cars around us. One hearse and one family car.

I am astonished. 40 years of service worked, multiple auxiliaries, Woman of the Year four times... one hearse and one family car. This soul had a sad beginning, a committed life, a miserable death, but no one else found the dignity to escort her remains to the burial grounds. So there, we sat as her body was committed to the ground. She finally met her parents and reunited with her siblings.

2 Corinthians 4:8-9

[8] We are troubled on every side, yet not distress; we are perplexed but not in despair [9] Persecuted, but not forsaken; cast down, but not destroyed in despair; [9] Persecuted, but not forsaken; cast down, but not destroyed;

You may not realize how resilient you are. Just look back over your countless battles; they did not destroy you. You are still here. You will mend. Once again, I refer you to the words of the Apostle Paul:

Philippians 4:11, "for I have learned in whatsoever state I am, therewith to be content."

Enjoy your solitude. The mind, soul, and spirit need rest. It is in the quiet times when God passes along your instruction, strength, and inspiration. Remember: When God breathed into Adam, Adam became a "living soul" Genesis2:7. The word 'breathe' in this context means inspiration (see the preface)

It is the breath of God that inspires us. Life and all goodness are enclosed in the breath of God. Adam was granted wisdom, knowledge, fellowship with God, and tremendous provisions - with the breath of God. Like many of you, my initial thought would be, "nothing is inspiring about suffering."

During the battle, it is not clear. However, Paul tells us in 2 Corinthians 12:1 - that suffering is a threshold to dreams and revelations of God.

The Ecclesiastical writer explains the normalcy of seasons:Ecclesiastes 3:1-9 King James Version (KJV) 3 To everything there is a season, and a time to every purpose underthe heaven: 2 A time to be born, and a time to die; a time toplant, and a time to pluck up that which is planted; 3 A timeto kill, and a time to heal; a time to break down, and a time

to build up (KJV).

Just as David turned to God with singing, worship, and prayers for mercy, they also left a list of blessings and Psalms of praise for the victories that followed suffering:

Psalm 116:1-5 1I love the LORD, because he hath heard my voice and my supplications. 2Because he hath inclined his ear unto me, therefore will I call upon him as long as I live. 3The sorrows of death compassed me, and the pains of hell gat hold upon me: I found trouble and sorrow. 4Then called I upon the name of the LORD; O LORD, I beseech thee, deliver my soul. 5Gracious is the LORD, and righteous; yea, our God is merciful.

These words are the key to suffering with a good spirit and a healthy attitude:

2 Corinthians 12:9 And he said unto me, My grace is sufficient for thee: for my strength is made perfect in weakness. Most gladly, therefore, will I rather glory in my infirmities, that the power of Christ may rest upon me.

What could be more valuable than the power of Christ resting on you?

2 Corinthians 12:1

"...I will come to visions and revelations of the Lord.

We all want the "visions and revelations," so we all must suffer.

BREATHE

Document and reflect on what trouble you the most.

_____

_____

_____

_____

_____

_____

_____

_____

_____

_____

_____

_____

_____

_____

_____

_____

_____

_____

_____

_____

_____

_____

What visions and revelations have you received from God?

_____

_____

_____

_____

_____

_____

_____

_____

_____

_____

_____

_____

_____

_____

_____

_____

_____

To appoint unto them that mourn in Zion, to give unto them beauty for ashes, the oil of joy for mourning, the garment of praise for the spirit of heaviness; that they might be called trees of righteousness, the planting of the LORD, thathe might be glorified. Isaiah 61:3.

BREATHE

Chapter 7 - The Tongue: Death of a Relationship
ANGER

AND AMONG ALL the parts of the body, the tongue is a flame of fire. It is a whole world of wickedness, corrupting your entire body. It can set your whole life on fire, for it is set on fire by hell itself. James 3:6 {NLT}

We were the best of friends. We had so much in common, both from middle-class two-parent homes. There were six children in our household and two in hers. Both sets of parents instilled a significant balance of church, education, social grace, dignity and self-respect in us. She and her sister were scholarly and lived on university campuses. My elder sisters were much more scholarly and sober than I, but we were Debutants, Junior Hostesses and took modeling lessons. Our parents were strict, so our faces were not be seen at the basement parties, and in the streets of the neighborhood after school, unless you were going to a local store, cleaners or visiting a friend in the same block, we lived in since all thefamilies knew each other.

Let's call her Vanessa. I met her on the job. We were both hired into a fortune 500 company in the Spring of 1979.

I was pretty timid coming on to the job. Barely out of high school, with some college credits under my belt, a professional acumen and living life as young people do. Excitement, fun, and adventure were always on the agenda. It seemed like most of the 200+ employees in this office were older and more experienced with life, so I was introverted. I lacked the confidence it took to engage in long conversations with any of them, fearing a psychological challenge or verbal sparring of some sort. People sought to gain respect with this display of indignation to establish a reputation of superiority. If they were friendly, I talked until break time was over or lunch ended.

The job was fine, and we made good money, so we dressed well. In those days, a reasonable collection of shoes from 9 West or The Wild Pair, a full-length leather coat in the winter, was a fashionable presentation. Always - absolutely always a great hairstyle, professionally done. These were the features of a young woman making her mark on the world. Well, Vanessa was such a person. We were about the same height, wore the same size clothing, the same complexion and our birthdays were just days apart. So we became friends. Shopping together, decorating our homes was inclusive of one another's taste, we hung out together a few times a week and usually worked the same shifts with the same off days. Two months after beginning the job, I got married. He knew she was a dear friend and at that age, I would make decisions of staying home or shopping or going to visit friends with Vanessa. After all, that's what friends do. We developed a great bond and trust. We shared secrets and favored each other's choices in companions and just wanted to see each other 'live the dream." In the real world, it is not that simple. Relationships have problems, families have flaws and in all honesty, we all make mistakes. This is what friends are for. We comforted each other in the bad times and hoped that life would return to normal, so we thought. This was the way life worked. And what we thought it was supposed to be was not reality. We were fine as friends and confidants. Never a harsh tone or disagreement. We even enjoyed the same musical artists so - I cannot tell you what happened to throw this friendship into crisis. Perhaps it was something I said, or something she did, whatever it was, a simple phone conversation erupted into a war of words, insults, and verbal assaults. Sparks turned into billowing flames. She quipped about my disastrous marriage, I retorted with her problemed relationships, she returned fire as I was reloaded. This went on several more rounds.

We went on and on – no one was there to stop us. I did hear her tell her sister to get out of her doorway because she was on the phone (she was at her parent's home). Verbally, we scratched, gouged, and cut each other into bloody shreds.

When we ran out of secrets and insults, refusing to hang up without the "crescendo" – there was silence.

We were silent for a moment, before uttering, "I don't have anything else to say to YOU." Of course, she let me know I was not important to her either. That was it. We hung up the phones. The entire time we had maintained our tone, as not to let on that we were striking nerves and inflicting pain. It was more like Clint Eastwood, we never yelled or released audible despair, but when I hung that phone up, I collapsed in tears.

My heart was broken. I thought she hated the fact that my marriage was troubled and that all the things we talked about had poured out of her as she was reading from a laundry list. Betrayed, embarrassed, demeaned, mocked, and scoffed at. She was my best friend. We had met years earlier, so by now, I was a manager for another fortune 500 company in a high-rise office building downtown and she had transferred to another position, so we did not have to see each other.

That exchange would sever our connection for almost 20 years.

She had gotten married and had two teenage children who were both beautiful and intelligent.

We talked and met for lunch even visited each other's homes, but the relationship was never the same. It was the kind of situation where you need to just keep your guard up, keep a watchful eye for body language and listen for innuendos or insinuations in each other's words. Finally, we were comfortable enough to relax. But it was never the same. Our words had done irreparable damage. Blame it on youth, hormone imbalance or pride. But a perfectly good friendship got out of control and forty years later, the dynamic is in ruins. One thing we did do that seemed to help was to apologize and acknowledge using personal information as weapons. I said, "Jennifer, when we hung up, I cried myself to sleep." She admitted crying as well, intensely. Fast forward 40 years, we have talked in the past several months, but it is not the same. The friendship is dead and waiting to be buried. Who knows, maybe we will connect again, and all will be forgiven? It could happen.

It Did Not Have to be This way

"An unruly member." The tongue sets on fire the courses of nature. So much damage is done simply with words. Thus, "life and death are in the power of the tongue." Proverbs 18:21 {KJV} Note: it, the tongue, "is set on fire by hell itself." The tongue is, when yielded, an instrument of hell. It uses the destructive power of fire. Whether scorched, singed, or utterly reduced to ashes, the tongue, when left unbridled, is ruthless.

It destroys homes, relationships, corporations, even rumors control the stock market, the tongue disassembles. "But the tongue can no man tame; it is an unruly evil, full of deadly poison." Clear acknowledgement that you, even with good intention and great effort, cannot control your own tongue. It will take the God of heaven to empower you.

We need not spend much time on this, but a moment of acknowledgement of guilt and repentance would open the way for forgiveness and empowerment. Start with words of acknowledgement, deep-seated honesty, followed by acknowledgement and the putting away of pride.

_____

_____

_____

_____

_____

_____

_____

_____

_____

_____

_____

_____

_____

_____

_____

_____

_____

_____

_____

It was the lack of control over the tongue that dismantled this relationship and left anger and apathy in the place of friendship. Anger continues to be a factor. Words matter.

Thankfully, when we reconcile with God, the relationship only gets better. He forgives, so we do not have to keep looking back.

With man, the past cannot be undone. Before saying something that you can never take back, or destroying somethingthat can never be replaced, take a moment to...

BREATHE

Chapter 8 - Living Your Best Life

SHOCK

SOME OF THE best years of my life were spent growing up with my mother. As far back as I could remember, my fondest memories are with her. I could remember her smiling while singing nursery rhymes, children's songs, and hymns. One funny memory I can recall was when I was sitting next to her one day and she picked up a mirror and said, "look at that pretty baby, "Confused, I looked on both sides to see what baby picture she was referring to. As a preteen, I grew to love her big toothy smile, so whenever I came home for lunch: I would tell her some good news or give her a flower I picked just for her.

As much as Sara, my mother smiled in my youth, inside she had not processed her grief. At the age of twelve, she was orphaned along with her thirteen siblings. Her unresolved grief surfaced when things in her life were going wrong. Consequently, she had two failed marriages, but in spite of them, she had nine beautiful children; three children from her second marriage and six from her third and final marriage to my father, Robert.

Even though we were many, that did not stop my mother from making our formative years filled with joy. Sometimes she would gather us around and just tell funny stories about her childhood in Buffalo. We listened intently, often laughing at her. She said someone told her she was like Lucille Ball. Oftentimes friends would come over and sit in the living room listening to her for long periods of time. It was a captivated audience and my friends all said she was beautiful.

Around the time I was in high school, mom was 49, stood about 5'5" and weighed about 125 pounds. She had a light complexion with hair long enough to lay on her back when braided. Her keen nose, thin lips and almond-shaped eyes made up the beauty that overrode the sadness within.

By the time we were all out of high school, her health began failing and hospital visits became frequent hospital stays. Mom was diagnosed with hypertension, diabetes, sickle-cell anemia, and cardiovascular disease. All of these diagnoses pushed her body into renal failure. By age 58, she opted to have cardiac surgery to correct arrhythmia that caused fainting spells and took her life. The heart surgery she had was to place an implantable defibrillator in her chest. This would automatically shock her heart back to a normal rhythm if she were to go into an arrhythmia attack. Arrhythmia is when the heart races, sometimes as high as 200 beats per minute. That is often fatal because, with that many beats, the heart is not fully contracting and pumping blood and oxygen through the body, depriving the organs of oxygen. Unless normal rhythm is restored, within moments, the patient could expire.

Hospital visits were increased to four to five times per year, then increased to bi-monthly. She was being held over for observation following dialysis when dad fell gravely ill. He passed that same night at Providence hospital. Who is going to tell mom? She is too sick to hear it over the phone. My brother David, the youngest of the nine children, said he would do it. No one challenged that. This one, the curly-headed baby that she referred to in infancy as 'God's only son.' If anyone could pass it on with care, David was best suited for the task. I remember going to the hospital after she received the news. She laid in the hospital bed, the room was silent, no television programs or music and she would not answer the phone. When I walked in and tried to comfort her, she just laid there with a blank expression. She would not talk. She was grieving.

Upon discharge, I went to the house and demanded she moved in with us. I was determined not to lose her and the only way to be sure of that was to take care of her. That meant monitoring her meals, medication, symptoms or signs of her co-morbidities. She had to be kept happy, because I never wanted to see her the way she looked after dad passed.

There were multiple episodes, even one time when she was dying and begged us not to take her to the hospital. This was the night EMS did not show up – so we picked her up, carried her to the car, laid her in the back seat and drove as fast as possible to get her to the nearest emergency room. We were stopped by the police. I explained, "my mother is dying' they turned on their lights and sirens and escorted us. They were kind enough to call ahead, which meant pulling up to awaiting medical team and a gurney.

Two hours later, I was called from the emergency waiting room to a small conference room. The doctor entered the room slowly. He appeared very puzzled - 'What happened?'

Me: She just wasn't feeling well and begged us not to take her to the hospital. When I saw how bad it was, we rushed her here. Where is she?

Doctor: You got here just in time. We gave her something tobring her blood pressure back up and she is responding now. Now, it is time to let the tears fall, I thought it was the end, but we still have her. My entire body was numb. I began to tremble until he said they brought her back. I was so thankful. I just lost dad two years ago. I will never let her get this bad again. That was the summer of 1992.

February 1993, another severe episode, we are not waiting for her to deteriorate. "Mom, we have to take you to the hospital." She looked so frightened. I was firm. You have to go and let them get this under control.

At some point after admission, my mother's potassium became so low. She began having arrhythmia attacks and the defibrillator in her chest began to fire off, shocking her heart to a normal rhythm. Unfortunately, the staff, including the attending physician, were oblivious to this device and how it functions. Due to the dialysis treatments, her potassium and other body chemistry were thrown off, so the defibrillator discharged again, and she passed out. They were at a loss. Thankfully, we arrived to find her in her room alone and regaining consciousness - she looked at me and pointed to her chest, then another jolt indicated to me that it had fired, so I told the attending physician.

That was when I called her attending physician at the hospital where the surgery was performed. They contacted staff and arranged for an ambulance to transfer her to them. This could not have been better. They resolved the pruitis (itching) likely caused by the dialysis fluids. They also regulated her vitals and brought her white blood count down, which is why she was disoriented. She was herself again, priceless. She asked me to sing, "He knows how much we can bear" she began singing and I joined in. She said I am enjoying the peace, no pain, no itching, no confusion. I am so thankful. It was Mother's Day 1993. Her long-time internal medicine physician walked into the room. I remembered him from my childhood. He said a few things that were very encouraging concerning her response to the treatment this hospital had provided.

Doctor: 'Unfortunately, we have to transfer her back because that is where her dialysis is provided. "She is very sick and probably does not have long."

Me: How long does she have?

Doctor: Maybe a week to 10 days.

I could not accept the idea of losing her for any reason and to hear this on Mother's Day brought down feelings of helplessness, fear and pity. I looked in the mirror and saw that my entire body had broken out in a rash. It was stress-related. This was destroying me in every way.

We made the most of that day. It was enjoyable and hopeful, then two days later, she was transferred back to Grace hospital, which in comparison, began to resemble a butcher shop. Within one week, the pruitis, high white blood count, disorientation and misery were all back. I spent as much time at the hospital as the nurses. Fortunately, my supervisor granted me an extended lunch daily so I could visit her. Otherwise, mom would not eat, only trusting me to feed her. After work, I would go directly to the hospital to feed her and to spend time with her before attending church. While at church, I was able to receive calls from the hospital. When church service was over, I returned to ensure she was comfortable for the night with no complications. I kept this schedule until the end of June. I was at mom's side for hours every day. I remember walking on the unit and hearing her calling for me. "Valerie, Valerie" - I am right here, mommy, what's wrong?

Mom: I am used to you being here at a certain time and when you are not here, I start calling for you.

Me: I will always be here, Mom. If you continue to stay stable, you may get discharged.

My mother was on her way to becoming discharged, so I began planning a homecoming party at the house. The front porch and house would be garnished with balloons and yellow ribbons. I wanted to bring closure to this chapter of her life and thought it warranted a loving and peaceful celebration.

After these five long and difficult months, she would love to be surrounded by her children, grandchildren, nieces, and nephews. Things went as well as could be expected and the discharge was set for Wednesday, July 7, 1993. At this time, I was a member of the Michigan State Youth Choir and we were invited to sing for an Independence Day service at the Church pastored by Bishop James A. Johnson in St. Louis Missouri, This would be a two-day trip and get me back early Monday with enough time to prepare the house for mom's celebration. I went to the hospital to visit her Friday as we were scheduled to be on the road before sunrise en route July 2nd to St. Louis.

It was a good visit; mom was coherent, and her pain was being managed. We were feeling good about the return to the house and having her in her own room again. On the way out the door, headed to the elevator, I said mom, I will be going to St. Louis tomorrow, but I will be back Monday. She told me she would be going home in two days. I responded, actually, mom, it will be five days, on Wednesday, so I will see you on Monday. She did not reply, I will see you on Monday, mommy... Okay? Bye, mom...

Mom: Bye

It was St. Louis tomorrow, but I will be back Monday. We made it to St. Louis late Saturday night. I remember the intense anointing that came over me when I prayed for my mother.

As the choir was singing, Bishop James A. Johnson asked one of the Mothers that chaperoned us on this trip if there was a preacher among the group.

Mother Ruth Mason: yes, right there (pointing me out), her name is Evangelist Valerie Jones.

Upon conclusion of the selection, he came over to me and asked,

Bishop: They told me you were a preacher, are you? Me: Yes, sir,

Bishop: Do you have your Bible?

Me: Yes, sir,

Bishop: I know this is God, but will you preach this morning sermon for us?

I looked around, approximately 1000 people in this congregation. This church was in an organization known for the powerful preachers that come out of it. I do not know anyone outside of those that traveled with us - Not even have a sermon prepared. But there was no indication that I should say no. I did not have an inclination to say no in my spirit. So, I replied. Okay.

The atmosphere was warm and receptive. As I approached the podium, a state of euphoria came over me. There was no fear. This euphoric feeling lasted throughout the sermon and ceased when I concluded the message and handed the service back over to Bishop Johnson.

This was a new milestone in my ministry. I could not wait to tell mom about this experience. The entire church was of stellar character - one by one, they embraced me and blessed me with words of encouragement. These words were like medicine to my spirit. I was worn down emotionally from watching my mother's suffering. Now I had good news to share with her like the old days.

We were treated to dinner and immediately set out for the 10-hour drive home. I pulled into my driveway at 3:45 a.m. I rang the doorbell and immediately heard my husband say, I will be right down, Val. He unloaded my luggage and said,we have to go to the hospital,

Me: WHY?

Him: Honey (mom's nickname) took a turn for the worst.

We jumped into the car arriving at the hospital just after 4 a.m. She was in ICU. I rushed into her room to find her on life support, we had been there before and she survived, so I had hope. One thing was different: her eyes were wide opened. She was looking up - non-responsive for hours, not even to blink and her corneas were drying out. I was struggling to imagine how bad it would get and when she would begin to turn around. Would she be blind? Would they be able to correct the damage to her eyes? The worst had already happened, and she would not be coming home to yellow balloons and flowers with ribbons. She had done exactly what she told me before I last left her bedside. She had gone home. But not in my heart. I was determined to continue believing it would get better as it always had. I would not give into what I was seeing. Even if it meant more episodes and more hours at the hospital, I wanted my mother.

The attending physician, an ICU nurse and a social worker watched me flounder for hours. Mom did not have a Power of Attorney (POA), but she lived with me, so my siblings were respectful of my role, the hospital was as well. My eldest sister, a Registered Nurse (RN), discreetly told me mom was not with us as she used to be. I took that with a grain of saltand only processed the words "as she used to be."

Concerning the staff, this had gone on long enough. The time had come to consult with the primary family members, the palliative care team, and ICU Staff. It was against my better judgement to leave the bedside. The need to discuss her status and everything they said just spiraled. I responded, but I was not giving in to the reality of death. They began to make different statements that were hard-hitting "that is not her breathing. It is the machines." – "There is no brain activity. You have to accept this." My husband insisted I take their words to heart. I ended the meeting by leaving the room, in so much despair. No one was understanding I was trying to wait on God.

My husband took me for a ride. I asked him, "What do you think is going to happen?" He just began to cry. We rode andcried for a good while.

At 6 pm that evening, with her children surrounding her, Sara Mitchell was removed from life support and the time of death Was called.

Failure! I had let everyone down. With all of my prayers, support and efforts, I had to tell mom's remaining siblings she was gone.

We were so close. She had suffered so much. She was scheduled to be discharged in two days – everything in me seemed to be melting into sorrow, disbelief, and heaviness. I cried.

The funeral was different, no tears.

My sisters and I wore yellow and white. Yellow roses with ribbons garnished her casket. It was a sunny day, so we had help from God to keep our heads lifted. During the repass, I handed my eldest sister Mom's beautiful wedding rings that dad gave her for their 25th wedding anniversary. Mom loved those rings. My sister was to pass them to her oldest daughter as an heirloom and ultimately many generations. By that evening, it rained pretty heavy. Mom and her siblings loved to sit outside and take in the fragrance and sound of rain. So soothing. My uncle Bill was the first to go outside. The porch had a large awning,

I followed and other family as well, sat quietly as the rain settled us. We just took time to.

BREATHE

Suffering is only effective when it corrects convictions, sharpens wisdom, and positively changes trajectories. The intense suffering is to bring about change. Your elevation is wrought through suffering. Just as the craft and shaping on the Potter's wheel, likewise, we are fashioned in the crucible of affliction. The intensity and discomfort come as the power of God rests on you in this process of forming and renewing. New wine requires new wineskins. Have hope in the end result. [read Romans 5:1-5]

The person that went into that test should in nowise continue or pick up where they left off to no degree. You have been changed. You have been raised up in power. You must move forward in a new dynamic, a new and living way.

Admonition:

God has not given us light to be in darkness or obscurity. He has not placed us in the body to flounder or struggle in hopelessness. He has not set us aside to debilitate or incapacitate us. There have been wounds, but He will heal them. He has taken us down to the brink of death but called us back. We are not just survivors. We are the called, the conquerors.

What has changed in your daily regiment following this experience?

_____

_____

_____

_____

_____

_____

_____

How important is it to you to do things God's way?

_____

_____

_____

_____

_____

_____

_____

_____

_____

How much of a role did the opinions and professionals play in your planning?

_____

_____

_____

_____

_____

_____

_____

_____

_____

_____

Are you a proponent of operating under your personal convictions?

_____

_____

_____

_____

_____

_____

_____

_____

_____

_____

What self-inflicted grief have you suffered? Begin with denial.

_____

_____

_____

_____

_____

_____

_____

_____

_____

_____

_____

Pause to contemplate: the seeds that you sow will protect your life. Seeds yield fruit after its own kind. Reflect:

_____

_____

_____

_____

_____

_____

_____

_____

_____

_____

_____

We sow to the wind and reap the whirlwind, Hosea 8:7 (KJV). It is the principle of planting a single grain of corn and receiving a harvest of an entire stalk with several ears of corn, and multiple grains of corn per ear. Sow good seeds always so you can ecstatically anticipate the whirlwind. Though painful, these were some of the best years of my life because I poured all I had into a soul that needed so much. The scripture on her obituary read:

For which cause we faint not: but though our outward man perish, yet the inward man is renewed day by day.

2 Corinthians 4:16 (KJV)

Mommy, breathe...

They that sow in tears shall reap in joy. Psalms 126:5 (KJV)

Chapter 9 - The Intervention

ACCEPTANCE

OUR CULTURE AND a large part of society dictates that it is improper for males to cry. In order to avoid that disapproval, men are taught from childhood to suppress grief. This is essentially a dumbing down of distress. Rather than compartmentalizing your emotions, try to understand how to process them.

Our society and culture would have done their due diligence if they allowed males to be taught from childhood that as they encounter adversity, they would experience a full range of emotions.

Suppressing, ignoring, or avoiding emotions is mismanagement of your spiritual being, and as a result, there is an eruption.

Consider a father and son experience I witnessed one night when I was on call. I walked into the emergency room, where a little boy was standing at the window speaking with a triage nurse. Meanwhile, his father stood behind him so the nurse could question the child, and the father could assist with answers as needed. Strategically, the parent is behind the child, so the child could speak with some semblance of candor. I noticed the child holding his head, struggling not to break down in tears. He was holding a cold, wet towel to his head that had blood on it. The impression said to me: he appeared terrified and in distress. It was clear the child was fighting tears. The father occasionally told him to speak up or speak clearly when responding to questions. I stood in the seating area to organize my documents, only to provide an opportunity to listen and see what was going on.

Finally, the nurse asked the child what happened - the child was not conveying it well enough, so the father said: "He fell on the trampoline and bumped his head."

I understood now, the injury occurred earlier, but the wound was still producing blood and the child was still in some level of distress. The decision was finally made to get it checked out at the hospital emergency room.

So many things went through my mind and heart: the pain of the initial impact, the fear a child gets when they see blood, and how long the child's head had been hurting before he was brought in for help.

At this stage of a child's life requires care, touch, listening and immediate relief. General attentiveness to be sure nothing unusual is happening. I did not hear the father say, do not cry, or you are okay, but the casual expression on his father's face and, the expression on the child's face were opposites.

The fact that they were in the emergency room made it clear that an injury which occurred hours earlier, finally resulted in an emergency room visit well after 1 a.m.

My prayers went out for this child. It is disheartening to see anyone in distress. In this case, the father was entrusted with the child's care, but mismanaged it. Most will agree with me here: no good parent would turn to a bleeding, crying child and say, "get over it," the type of council or cajoling some people offer. This is obviously not the way to manage pain.

Consider this spiritual crisis intervention.

It is equally important to properly acknowledge the injury, provide relief while it hurts worst: beginning with the anxiety while you are waiting for the pain medication to begin taking effect. Breathing exercises work very well in calming and stabilizing. Simply make a few statements and as they listen, they will begin to compose themselves because they are focusing on what is being said. What is being said must be relevant, substantive and spoken with care. Use a peaceful, confident tone to defray the fretfulness and give them a moment to just breathe.

BREATHE

This is obviously not the way to manage pain.

Consider this spiritual crisis intervention:

It slows the heart rate, helps regulate respiration and lowers cortisol levels while allowing time for the mind to settle.

Now the setting is more suitable for inquiry and discussion with rationality.

Now twice victimized; first by the incident and secondly, by mismanagement, it becomes radically critical for the informed, careful intervention to occur. There is always a learning period, but never a need to justify an ineffective practice when options are discoverable. Not all mismanagement is malicious. Often it comes down to a crude reality; someone here failed to choose a proper plan of action or plan of care.

Q: What is the solution?:

A: Get acquainted. Learn from your suffering how to help others.

BREATHE

Chapter 10 - Get Acquainted

ACCEPTANCE

"THOU COMPASSEST MY path and my lying down, and art acquainted with all my ways." Psalms 139:3 (KJV)

Likewise, we need to be acquainted with all our ways. No one wants to be unpopular. It breeds disrespect, and in even less mature characters, it encourages bullying. Even the most timid person may find the courage to take a verbal swipe at you if they see you are disliked. Psychological bullying, verbal abuse, and embarrassment can reduce an individual to anger; and low self-esteem. They may believe the best way to counter it is to relinquish their integrity and give in to the demands of the antagonist.

Once I worked with a young man that was well respected but cowered at the tone the manager tended to take with employees. The manager stood about 5'3' with a medium to small build, had a receding hairline and was pretty ordinary in appearance. But this was the way he garnered submission and adherence from his subordinates. The employee that avoided him was a young man with a very decent education. He was considered attractive and successful in the office. But when asked why he shuttered at the threat of being talked down to, even for the slightest reason, he responded. "I don't have broad shoulders." Neither did the antagonist, but his unethical approach to management style worked.

To secure his position, he used manipulation, brown-nosing, and apple polishing to work his way up the ladder.

In order to continue enjoying success, he would have to continue this juvenile behavior. How much intelligence does it really take to verbally shove people around? After all, the fate of your subordinate's livelihoods was within your scope of authority.

People may be willing to endure difficult relationships, but this is one of the most trying, because it challenges your pride and integrity. If a breach is allowed past the appropriate boundaries, it may trigger a negative reaction from you. Oftentimes, pride and resentment may control your reactions. To contend with this challenge intelligently and with civility is a major achievement.

Otherwise, a toxic pattern of mismanaging relationships and abuse of authority are formed and fortified. When it comes to public humiliation and disrespect, some will cower. In the end, it is better to be despised by people than to violate your conscience and decimate your moral foundation. Celebrate your integrity and unshakeable determination. Persevere harshness and retain healthy self-esteem.

Moses was often chided and criticized, and his authority was challenged, but he was not moved to intimidation.

Paul was a man that was physically punished for staying on course, as unpopular as it was. Jesus Himself, came to His own people to be called filth and liar, to be physically picked up by a hateful crowd with the intention of throwing Him over a cliff.

What was the grief and sorrow Jesus bore and became acquainted with? It is written that He was tempted and suffered the very things we do. It was necessary. It made Him compassionate and just, not a respecter of persons. You will never be torn down, but always build up because He has suffered in such a way that compassion supersedes all other factors.

Getting acquainted with unpleasant experiences smooths rough edges in the soul. Some may have walked off jobs - ending their employment with the intent of escaping conflict. As long as you are in this world, there will be trouble to contend with. It is important to stand up to challenges God's way, so that when we arrive at these mountains, we arrive inhumility and without guilt.

As we get acquainted with grief, I ask you to have hope that your understanding will be enlightened for the sake of my calling.

Your anointing, which is your enablement, is as unique as your fingerprint. Not being controlled by others is of utmost importance, remember, they themselves are accountable for their decisions to be integral. Where is the application?

This is a lesson in meekness and strength.

Meek - quiet, gentle, easily imposed upon. (Oxford Language)

How to Get Acquainted

Clinical Pastoral Education was, of all my learning experiences, in this life-long-learning journey, the most valuable. The more meaningful discovery occurred and will remain with me for life.

I explored territory where, [for the sake of metaphoric graphics] the terrain was rough, roads were untreated and, in some areas, the roads were unpassable. Clinical Pastoral Education was dual purposed; self-examination juxtaposed to patient and family care.

The requirement was not to assess the patient or family based on their behavior, but on mine. What if the shoe were on the other foot? Has the shoe ever been on the other foot? During interventions and even during self-care, ask yourself; is there anything familiar about this situation? Have I ever been here or even felt this way?

In the summer of 1978, at Clinton Street Greater Bethlehem Temple Church attending my paternal grandmother's funeral, one of the worst experiences of my life was about to unfold.

My grandmother used to bring me here as a child. I always spent weekends and summers with her even though my immediate family lived on the other side of town, but moments from the church. Her death was no surprise. She had been ill for months and declining, so when death came, it was comforting to know that everything she lived for was realized, she was now in the presence of the Lord.

As I recall, I may have shed few tears after passing the open casket. That was to be expected. What was NOT expected was the outburst of pleading with the funeral director. He proceeded to close the casket. "Please don't close it, please!" They paused momentarily, the soloist, who had just beautifully rendered, Tremaine Hawkins' "I'm Going Up Yonder," rushed over and beckoned to me to come to her; she was going to minister to me at my grandmother's side before they closed the casket. I was frozen. She was gone, and no one could do anything about it. I was temporarily inconsolable.

I was as stunned as anyone present, but with the comfort of my father and sisters, I was able to accept the finality of her earthly existence. This sharp emotional pain stayed with me. I looked around to see if anyone was in as much unbelief as me. I observed bowed heads, some were wiping away tears and others were taking in the services and the closing of the casket.

From just a row ahead of me, cajoled by the glaring eyes of one of my elder cousins, it was clear that he was demanding I tone it down a few notches. It was not acceptable behavior. This is the way grief acts. Often unexpected behavior - met with disapproval. There must be common ground when the pendulum swings from one side to the other. Everyone is accountable in this context,

According to Dr. Afzel Beemath {2014}, palliative care physician, everyone has the same accountability, doctors, pastors, chaplains, other clinicians and ancillary professionals – that accountability being: "use a pliable approach." When it comes to approaches, "it is all psychological." In this interview, Beemath adds:

BREATHE

Entering a scenario, event, or crisis, the approach should be aligned to the atmosphere. If there is laughter – a solemn approach would be improper. The same is true if the atmosphere is calm. Use the correct approach. This evokes trust and confidence that your approach will make your presence matter, people will be more accepting of you. Talk in simple terms so that people get it. Avoid terminology that could distance you from the listeners. There will be times when we mess up. All is not lost - how can you recover, is the strategy to apply. (Beemath, 2014)

BREATHE

It is necessary for you to experience the full range of emotions, examine them and their impact and your own coping strategies. You will, in turn, be a better father, husband, brother, pastor, sibling, friend, and colleague. When they need you, they need to know that you care, because you have the experience that helps you to understand. This is what makes Jesus the great high priest that he is:

Hebrews 2:17 For this reason, he had to be made like them, fully human in every way, in order that he might become a merciful and faithful high priest in service to God, and that he might make atonement for the sins of the people.

Isaiah 53 tells us Jesus was a man of sorrows and acquainted with grief. Getting acquainted with grief is of great benefit.

His visage was marred more than any man – this was a visual of the extent of acquaintance he had with physical pain. He was mutilated. As extensive as his physical injuries were, we must conclude; the inward man, mind, soul, and spirit were likely acquainted. The equivalent of spiritual mutilation was His experience. It was extreme and beyond human comprehension. He was acquainted for the express purpose of empathy and infinite understanding.

To benefit others, we need to be acquainted, because your life is fraught with experiences. Examine them. Parse your thoughts carefully. Chances are, you are not in uncharted territory. There are parallels. You survived perils. Remember those unpassable roads, and rough terrain. They are all behind you. It will help sustain you. You will be of more value to the kingdom assignment on your life. Get acquainted.

BREATHE

Chapter 11 - Confrontation Phase

DENIAL TO ACCEPTANCE

CONFRONTATION IS THE polar opposite of ignoring or dismissing grief.

It is equal to hiding from a bully, hoping they will go away, versus standing up for yourself. What this is really doing is putting it off.

Confrontation is the process of mentally processing what has happened and permitting the grief process to organically occur. Otherwise, grief presents itself intrusively and can be unmanageable. Ask the typical male how they cope with grief. Essentially, you will learn they give it a space of time; usually the initial event, followed by a funeral and conclude the public process there. Most of the time, it is because they do not see the value of crying and being emotional in fear, they will lose control. This is a sense of being debilitated, something no male willingly opens themselves to. They have learned to endure in privacy.

For some, emotions are viewed as weakness, which is erroneous. There are at least 10 basic emotions: happiness, sadness, anger, anticipation, fear, loneliness, jealousy, disgust, surprise, trust. These are all emotions, that are triggered by events and memories in our lives daily. Why should sadness be categorized as a sign of weakness, while other emotions like "surprise" and "trust" are eagerly anticipated or worn as a badge of honor? Possibly because sadness evokes tears and tears cause males to appear debilitated, according to society.

Your thoughts...

_____

_____

_____

_____

_____

_____

_____

_____

_____

_____

_____

_____

_____

_____

_____

_____

_____

_____

_____

_____

_____

_____

_____

_____

_____

_____

_____

_____

_____

_____

_____

_____

_____

_____

    Emotions inform us of the impact life's events have on us. Were the events a result of personal mistakes, for the sake of learning by experience or an opportunity to utilize strengths? Survival and endurance are evidence of strength, with or without tears or sadness. Understand these triggers - lead to finding coping strategies. {for more reading on emotions, read the online article: 10 Basic Emotions and What They'reTrying to Tell You} (Chloe, 2020)

Chapter 12 - Compartmentalizing Grief
DENIAL

THE BOOK OF Nehemiah lays open the path of grief from beginning to end. His method was clear:

After the exile, Nehemiah, like many other Jews, continued their existing living arrangements and livelihoods because Jerusalem was still in ruins as a result of the pillaging that occurred when they were taken captive. His role was to serve the King as cupbearer.

Nehemiah's grief was triggered by bad news. All he wanted to know was how everyone back in Jerusalem was doing. He asked this question to some of his brethren: "How are our brethren in Jerusalem?" The reply was that they were in great despair and that the city laid in ruins. (Nehemiah chapter one)

He grieved so deeply that when it was time to go to work there before the king in the palace, he was unable to put up a façade. The King was smitten by the visible affliction of Nehemiah's heart and asked why he was so afflicted. It was obviously not a physical malady, but as the King said: "...This is nothing but sorrow of the heart." Nehemiah 2:2 (KJV). Of course, Nehemiah was terrified that he appeared to be in some level of trauma. He was the King's cupbearer, wine-taster, or the one that made sure the King was not being poisoned. It was reasonable for the King to be concerned, even for his own safety.

It was divine order. Nehemiah took grief into a private place and wept, grieving deeply. Then he fasted: this was to lift the heaviness and so he could petition God for help. The day he appeared before the King in distress was following his prayer and fasting. Sometimes relief does not come right away; prayer should not be expected to instantaneously erase sorrow, but it may. However, after the unloading his heaviness with prayer, weeping, and fasting, he sought for a solution.

When the King asked about this "sorrow of the heart: Nehemiah presented his request - it was to take leave and go to Jerusalem to help rebuild the city. That was Nehemiah's solution. With all favor from the King, he went and did just as he requested. Coping strategies are your solutions. Addressing the problem with solutions.

Finish a project, contributed to a program, offer your support, yield your gifts. Use the passion, be driven by desire;

it will make the task easier and rewarding. They can rebuild the walls of your heart and life that seem to lay in ruins and cast light on brighter thoughts. The gift of life is to live it to the fullest and this path is clear.

Managing spiritual pain in this tool is done by first acknowledging or giving credence to your pain, then grieve - cry if you have to then, find a way to cope or resolve the reason you are grieving. Putting it away or setting it aside, with the notion that it has been given the necessary attention and you have concluded the matter.

This is true, until it is not! The mind and body have a way of coping with grief or numbing the pain.

This is a list of options that many have taken to cope with grief, including alcohol in access, illicit drug use, stimulants, opioids, radical - thrill-seeking behaviors, binge eating, frivolous physical conduct, such as sexual misconduct and violence.

On the other hand, there is a list that drives unresolved grief: stress, depression, anxiety, loss of sleep, a decline in socialization, and loss of appetite. All of the above endanger the body with chronic illness, serious disease or worse. Grief must be confronted, faced, addressed and coping strategies must be employed.

Disenfranchised Grief - Forced to Compartmentalize

This occurs when grief is disregarded, unrecognized or deemed illegitimate. This is improper and forces others to suffer in silence: which is neither Christian, Kingdom, nor healthy.

Per Romans 12:15, "rejoice with those who rejoice and mourn with them that mourn. It is part of the human experience. Disenfranchised grief is an offense to this scripture, moreover, an offense to God.

The expression "You are wearing your feelings on your shoulders" signifies weakness, inadequate coping and suggests the concern is insignificant. God's ways are not our ways. It may not be inadequate to "Take heed to yourselves..."Luke 21:36 (KJV) - What are you allowing?

We played the pipe for you, and you did not dance; we sang a dirge, and you did not mourn.' 18 For John came neither eating nor drinking, and they say, 'He has a demon.' 19 The Son of Man came eating and drinking, and they say, 'Here is a glutton and a drunkard, a friend of tax collectors and sinners.' But wisdom is proved right by her deeds."

Perhaps to some degree, it may appear to be a case of weakness. Wisdom suggests we consider the cause of the person's spiritual pain. Then it becomes possible and likely that something can be done about it. Be the ointment. Wisdom isillustrated in deeds.

People are suffering in these astonishing times. Dignity and compassion should be the order of the day. Sending someone away worse than when they came suggests: the pain and your grief is unresolved.

Compartmentalize it! Moreover, it would leave the impression that you are not giving credence to their plight and are unconcerned.

Not Good!

When Jesus speaks in this passage, He speaks from the position of the 1st person, indicating it is experiential to Him. "a high priest touched by the feeling of our infirmities." As much as Jesus was tempted in all points like as we, yet without- out sin; consider, His agony was discarded. His tears were shrugged off by others, his words of heaviness fell on deaf ears. We are very much human; humanity has been flawed by sin.

In another passage, Jesus hones attention on to the nature of man:

Luke 11: 13 - Multiple versions

"If you then, being evil, know how to give good gifts unto your children: how much more shall your heavenly Father give the Holy Spirit to them that ask him? (KJV)."

As bad as you are, you know how to give good things to your children. How much more, then, will the Father in heaven give the Holy Spirit to those who ask him!" Good News Translation

If you then, with all your human frailty, know how to give your children gifts that are good for them, how much more certainly will your Father who is in Heaven give the Holy Spirit to those who ask Him!" Weymouth New Testament translation.

The focus is on human capability. It is inadequate with tendencies of being evil. But of course, God's ways are more than superior to ours. This is sustained by the words of the prophet Isaiah, chapter 49:15:

Can a woman forget her sucking (nursing) child, that she should not have compassion on the son of her womb? Even these may forget, yet I will not forget you.

We are not the Chief Shepherd, but we answer to Him regarding the care and well-being of the sheep. Even in this, we do not approach the matter with fear of mismanagement, but with the heart of a servant and the love of Jesus, knowing that our day is coming. I have lived long enough to remember the hushing and shutting-down of cries for justice concerning difficult home- lives spawned by inherent teaching. The leaders or teachers simply handed down what was handed to them and what they genuinely believed to be fundamental and orderly. Oh, how they erred, sending women to the corners with their complaints and continue suffering in silence.

We have a Great High Priest.

He works in two specific ways concerning our pain: He as He resolves our pain, and He teaches others, through pain, how to console. Whichever side of this process you are on, He is our Great High Priest. No human personality or human wisdom is comparable. Continue with confidence in Him alone.

So now I am giving you a new commandment: Love each other. Just as I have loved you, you should love each other.

Let us do it God's way so we can...
BREATHE

Chapter 13 - Coping Mechanisms and Strategies

COPING MECHANISMS

THE BODY INNATELY attends to stress subconsciously. There are hormones and enzymes in glands in the body that are involuntarily released in response to stresses around us.

These are just reminders of what the book has delineated in stories, outcomes from factual research and scripture. For a more expansive explanation of coping with grief, see volume 2 of this "Spiritual Pain Management Series" (see the last page of this book)

Healthy Coping Mechanisms

Breathe: Practice taking deep breaths to calm and relax your body.

Write Down Your Feelings: All of that anger and frustration can be written out. Journaling helps to relive the experience, in hindsight and unload unprocessed grief.

Call a Friend: Have a couple of close friends that know and understand your situation. Call them when you need someone to listen. This should transition into self-sufficiency as you continue journaling.

Regular exercise, such as running, or team sports, is a good way to handle the stress, given the situation.

Meditating on pleasant things and the Word of God are always beneficial, both spiritually and physically.

Progressive muscle relaxation. Be aware of tensed shoulders, poor posture and long periods of being immobile. Move around a bit and stretch. These among other techniques of relaxation.

Thinking it through on your own is an opportunity for the body and mind to share the task of releasing anxiety. The brain knows when to dispatch neurotransmitters to that will trigger specific glands in the body to release hormones or enzymes that work like medicine to defray this urgency and calm you.

This practice will permit you to strengthen your ability to gauge and reduce grief, even if it is just until additional help is available.

BREATHE

If this work has helped you in any way, please pass it on tohelp others.

Purchase this book as a gift for someone who needs it.

Please write a review that will encourage someone to get help.

Watch for the next volume in this series to be released in early 2021.

Spiritual Pain Management Series©

Appendix A

DISENFRANCHISED GRIEF

Disenfranchised grief, also known as hidden grief or sorrow, refers to any grief that goes unacknowledged or invalidated by social norms. This kind of grief is often minimized or not understood by others, which makes it particularly hard to process and work through.

Appendix B

TERMS

Anticipatory Grief - Anticipatory grief is defined as grief that occurs before death (or another great loss) in contrast to grief after death {conventional grief}.

Bereavement - comes from the same Latin root word as "to have been robbed, " i.e., to have experienced loss {Doka,2008}.

Clinical Pastoral Education - Clinical pastoral education {CPE} programs train chaplains to engage patients and their loved ones in cathartic discussions, establish rapport while maintaining eye contact, paying attention, and responding to both verbal and non-verbal cues to better understand what the observations during sessions. {Association of Clinical Pastoral Education {ACPE}.

Disenfranchised Grief - Grief that persons experience when they incur a loss that is not or cannot be openly acknowledged, socially sanctioned or publicly mourned".

Unresolved Grief - Grief characterized by the extended duration of the symptoms, by the interference of the grief symptoms with the normal functioning of the mourner, and/or by the intensity of the symptoms {for example, intense suicidalthoughts or acts}

Complicated Grief - Seven symptoms constitute complicated grief: searching, yearning, preoccupation with thoughts of the deceased, crying, disbelief regarding the death, feel- ing stunned by the death, lack of acceptance of the death (Prigerson, 1995, pp.)

Grieving Parameters - identifiers of the range and characteristics typical to one's personality and coping preferences.Delayed Grief - In cases of delayed grief, the reaction to the loss is postponed until a later time, even years later, andmight be triggered by a seemingly unrelated event, such as arecent divorce or even the death of a pet, but with reactions excessive to the current situation.

Appendix C

FIVE STAGES OF GRIEF

Denial

Denial is the stage that can initially help you survive the loss. You might think life makes no sense, has no meaning, and is too overwhelming. You start to deny the news and, in effect, go numb. It's common in this stage to wonder how life will go on in this different state - you are in a state of shock because life as you once knew it has changed in an instant. If you were diagnosed with a deadly disease, you might believe the news is incorrect – a mistake must have occurred somewhere in the lab-they mixed up your blood work with someone else. If you receive news on the death of a loved one, perhaps you cling to a false hope that they identified the wrong person. In the denial stage, you are not living in 'actual reality,' rather, you are living in a 'preferable' reality. Interestingly, it is denial and shock that help you cope and survive the grief event. Denial aids in pacing your feelings of grief. Instead of becoming completely overwhelmed with grief, we deny it, do not accept it, and stagger its full impact on us at one time. Think of it as your body's natural defense mechanism saying, "Hey, there's only so much I can handle at once." Once the denial and shock starts to fade, the start of the healing process begins. At this point, those feelings thatyou were once suppressing are coming to the surface.

Anger

Once you start to live in 'actual' reality again and not in 'preferred' reality, anger might start to set in. This is a common stage to think, "why me?" and "life's not fair!" You might look to blame others for the cause of your grief and also may redirect your anger to close friends and family. You find it incomprehensible how something like this could happen to you. If you are strong in faith, you might start to question your belief in God. "Where is God? Why didn't he protect me?" Researchers and mental health professionals agree that this anger is a necessary stage of grief. And encourage anger. It's important to truly feel the anger. It's thought that even though you might seem like you are in an endless cycle of anger, it will dissipate – and the more you truly feel the anger, the more quickly it will dissipate, and the more quickly you will heal. It is not healthy to suppress your feelings of anger – it is a natural response – and perhaps, arguably, a necessary one. In everyday life, we are normally told to control our anger toward situations and toward others. When you experience a grief event, you might feel disconnected from reality – that you have no grounding anymore. Your life has shattered and there's nothing solid to hold onto. Think of anger as a strength to bind you to reality. You might feel deserted or abandoned during a grief event. That no one is there. You are alone in this world. The direction of anger toward something or somebody is what might bridge you back to reality and connect you to people again. It is a "thing." It's something to grasp onto – a natural step in healing.

Bargaining

When something bad happens, have you ever caught yourself making a deal with God? "Please God, if you heal my husband, I will strive to be the best wife I can ever be – and never complain again." This is bargaining. In a way, this stage is false hope. You might falsely make yourself believe that you can avoid the grief through a type of negotiation. If you change this, I'll change that. You are so desperate to get your life back to how it was before the grief event. You are willing to make a major life change in an attempt toward normality. Guilt is a common wingman of bargaining. This is when you endure the endless "what if" statements. What if I had left the house 5 minutes sooner – the accident would have never happened. What if I encouraged him to go to the doctor six months ago like I first thought - the cancer could have been found sooner and he could have been saved.

Depression

Depression is a commonly accepted form of grief. In fact, most people associate depression immediately with grief – as it is a "present" emotion. It represents the emptiness we feel when we are living in reality and realize the person or situation is gone or over. In this stage, you might withdraw from life, feel numb, live in a fog, and not want to get out of bed. The world might seem too much and too overwhelming for you to face. You don't want to be around others, don't feel like talking, and experience feelings of hopelessness. You might even experience suicidal thoughts - thinking, "what's the point of going on?"

Acceptance

The last stage of grief identified by Kubler-Ross is acceptance. Not in the sense that "it's okay my husband died" rather, "my husband died, but I'm going to be okay." In this stage, your emotions may begin to stabilize. You re-enter reality. You come to terms with the fact that the "new" reality is that your partner is never coming back – or that you are going to succumb to your illness and die soon – and you're okay with that. It's not a "good" thing – but it's something you can live with. It is definitely a time of adjustment and readjustment. There are good days, there are bad days, and then there are good days again. In this stage, it does not mean you'll never have another bad day – where you are uncontrollably sad. But the good days tend to outnumber the bad days. In this stage, you may lift from your fog, you start to engage with friends again, and you might even make new relationships as time goes on. You understand your loved one can never be replaced, but you move, grow, and evolve into your new reality.

BREATHE

References

Burke, L. A., Niemeyer, R. A., & McDevitt-Murphy, M. E. {2010}. African American homicide bereavement: Aspects of social support that predict complicated grief, PTSD, and depression. OMEGA-Journal of death and dying, 61(1), 1-24.

Chloe, {2020} Psych2GO "10 Basic Emotions and What They're Trying to Tell You, online article, retrieved November 2020, https://psych2go.net/10-basic-emotions-and-what- they're-trying-to-tell-you/

Corr, C. {2001}. VIOLENCE AND UNEXPECTED DEATH. Partnership for Caring Inc. http://webpages.scu. edu/ftp/fow/pages/ course/c-13.html. Para 2

Gregory, Christina Ph.D. "An Examination of the Kubler-Ross Model. Psycom, September 23, 2020. www.psycom. net depression.central.grief.html

McCall T. (2011) New York: "Yoga as Medicine" Bantem Dell a Division of Random House Inc, online PDF, retrieved November 2020. Researchgate.net

Scaccia, Annmarya, (2020) "Serotonin: What You Need to Know," healthline.com, retrieved online December 4, 2020. www.healthline.com/health/mental-health/serotonin

Simpson, Valerie (2016) "Walking with Persons in Grief" Doctoral Dissertation, ProQuest archives, enzineArticles. com10404155

Prigerson, H. (1995, January 1). "Complicated Grief and Bereavement Related." Retrieved December 26, 2014, http://cat.inist.fr/?aModele+affiche&cpsidt=343554

Made in the USA
Monee, IL
17 November 2021